Presented by:

First Presbyterian Church, Peru

Presented to:

Meg Guthrie

Date:

May 24, 2009

This day and your life are God's gift to you:
so give thanks and be joyful always!
JIM BEGGS

I'M A GRADUATE NOW WHAT?

STEP INTO

YOUR **FUTURE**—

LIVE OUT

YOUR **DREAMS**

HOWARD BOOKS
A DIVISION OF SIMON & SCHUSTER
New York   London   Toronto   Sydney

Our purpose at Howard Books is to:
- Increase faith in the hearts of growing Christians
- Inspire holiness in the lives of believers
- Instill hope in the hearts of struggling people everywhere

Because He's coming again!

HOWARD
BOOKS

Published by Howard Books, a division of Simon & Schuster, Inc.
1230 Avenue of the Americas, New York, NY 10020
www.howardpublishing.com

I'm a Graduate . . . Now What? Step Into Your Future—Live Out Your Dreams
Copyright © 2008 by Dave Bordon and Associates, LLC

ISBN-13: 978-1-4165-8916-7
ISBN-10:   1-4165-8916-3

10 9 8 7 6 5 4 3 2 1

HOWARD and colophon are a registered trademarks of Simon & Schuster, Inc.

Manufactured in the United States of America

For information regarding special discounts for bulk purchases, please contact: Simon & Schuster Special Sales at 1-800-456-6798 or business@simonandschuster.com.

Project developed by Bordon Books, Tulsa, Oklahoma
Project writing and compilation by Sheila Seifert and Rebecca Currington in association with Snapdragon Group℠ Editorial Services.
Edited by Chrys Howard
Cover design by Lookout Design

The quoted ideas expressed in this book (other than Scripture verses) are not, in all cases, exact quotations, as some have been edited for clarity and brevity. In all cases, the author has attempted to maintain the speaker's original intent. In some cases, quoted material for this book was obtained from secondary sources, primarily print media. While every effort was made to ensure the accuracy of these sources, the accuracy cannot be guaranteed. For additions, deletions, corrections, or clarifications in future editions of this text, please contact the Publisher.

CONTENTS

Life is but one continual course
of instruction.
R. HILL

The main part of intellectual education is
not the acquisition of facts but learning
how to make facts live.
OLIVER WENDELL HOLMES JR.
twentieth-century American jurist

INTRODUCTION

Your graduation is a momentous occasion. It signals a sort of coming of age, a milestone, an awesome achievement—but how about life after graduation? What now?

As you move into the next phase of your life, you will need inspiration and motivation, affirmation of your character, priorities, and values and loads of helpful information to help you build a life on the far side of your formal education. That's what this book is all about.

I'm a Graduate . . . Now What? was designed to get you started on your way—it's the real lowdown for the real world. We pray that the true stories, inspirational quotations and poems, motivational speeches, letters and profiles, and practical, accessible advice will prove to be a valuable resource for the journey ahead.

This time, like other times, is a very good one,
if we but know what to do with it.

RALPH WALDO EMERSON
nineteenth-century American essayist and poet

SAY YES TO YOUR ACHIEVEMENTS

Celebrating How Far You've Come

*Enjoy your achievements
as well as your plans.*
MAX EHRMANN
twentieth-century idealist and philosopher

*I have fought a good fight, I have
finished my course, I have kept the faith.*
2 TIMOTHY 4:7 KJV

Meet the Dream Weavers

*[From space] the stars don't look
bigger, but they do look brighter.*

Sally Ride

Many young men and women fantasize about becoming astronauts.
Few ever achieve that dream. So isn't it even more unusual that the first
American female astronaut snagged the job on little more than a whim?

All her life, Sally Ride proved she was a woman of ability and high
achievement. At age ten, the Southern California native began playing
tennis. She loved it and eventually earned national recognition as a junior
tennis player.

Following high school, she went off to college, but she missed her
days in tennis and soon decided to pursue a professional tennis career
instead. After realizing her hard work wasn't enough to compete on the
professional level, Ride returned to school. She graduated from Stanford
University with bachelors' degrees in both English and physics, as well as a
master of science in physics, and then remained at the school to pursue a
doctorate.

Then on a fateful day in 1977, she picked up the Stanford University
newspaper and read about NASA's search for astronauts. Here's where
it gets good! On a whim, she applied for their training program and
was accepted—one of six women chosen from almost nine thousand
applicants.

The next year, Ride began preparing for assignment to a future space-
shuttle crew. On June 18, 1983, she served as a Mission Specialist for the
space shuttle's seventh mission, and she later flew a second time on the
same *Challenger* space shuttle.

In 1986, while Ride was preparing for her third flight, the *Challenger* tragically blew up in space. Shortly thereafter, Ride was appointed to a presidential commission investigating the accident. After the *Columbia* shuttle accident of 2003, she again served on the investigation commission—the only person appointed to both commissions.

Sally Ride retired from NASA in 1987 and spent the next few years teaching at Stanford and the University of California at San Diego.

In 2001 she formed Sally Ride Science, a company helping girls and young women pursue careers in science, math, and technology. Dr. Ride has also written five science books for children.

Not bad for a tennis player who applied for space travel on a whim.

Call to me and I will answer you and tell you great
and unsearchable things you do not know.
JEREMIAH 33:3

THE POWER OF POTENTIAL

What do you hope to achieve in your lifetime? Think and pray about your dreams and then put them down on paper. When you do, you'll be taking the first step to dressing your dreams in reality.

If God simply handed us everything we wanted, he would be taking from us our greatest prize—the joy of achievement.

VERN MCLELLAN
twenty-first-century editor

3

A Valedictorian Address

Edith Painton
American writer

Dear Friends, One and All:

They say there are people who always like to have the last word. I am sure I cannot see why they should, for to me it seems the hardest of all words to say, and I would rather somebody else should be the one to say it. For that last word must be, to many if not all of us, "Good-bye!"

We have finished the course that has been given us, and are now ready for a step forward along the pathway of life. So far we have come together, hand in hand, and we have been looking forward to this time as a glad one, forgetting that it was going to mean a time of parting. Now we are suddenly forced to remember this feature, and in spite of our triumph, it makes us sad. We did not realize how hard it was going to be to say it, did we? In our work here together, we have become very dear friends, and it is always hard to say good-bye, even for a little time, to the ones we have learned to care for. We have shared our pleasures, our triumphs and our few disappointments for so long that we shall miss the old companionship more than we now realize, when we are too far apart to enjoy it any longer. It is pleasant to pause here at the bending of the stream, and consider for a little the pleasant calmness of the wave-ripples through which we have so easily been rowing; but we cannot linger long, for already the noise of life's larger waters is calling us, and we know that we must row ahead out of the peaceful, shallow current of our . . . life, where we have been able to drift through so much of our passage, and pull hard through the deeper channels against the stream of an active life.

Dear Parents, Guardians and Friends, we cannot pass forever out of this quiet channel into the deeper waters awaiting us, without thanking you from the bottom of our hearts for the privilege of beginning this voyage of life on the breast of so clear and calm a stream. To you, dear teachers, we must also express our earnest thanks . . . and thus, classmates, we . . . face every duty of the unknown waters bravely and boldly, the principles of honor ever turning the pilot-wheel, as we sail to the success no graduate . . . can ever fail to win.[1]

The best educated human being is the one who understands most about the life in which he is placed.

HELEN KELLER
twentieth-century American deafblind lecturer and author

THE POWER OF POTENTIAL

Don't wait for life to come to you. Meet it head-on. Start actively looking for ways to achieve your dreams. Keep a journal where you can jot down ideas and information that might help you along the way.

Wear your learning like your watch, in a private pocket; and do not pull it out, and strike it, merely to show that you have one.

PHILIP STANHOPE, 4TH EARL OF CHESTERFIELD
eighteenth-century British statesman and author

ATTITUDES OF ACHIEVEMENT

★ *The reward of a thing well done is to have done it.*
RALPH WALDO EMERSON, *nineteenth-century American essayist and poet*

★ *To achieve great things we must live as though we were never going to die.*
MARQUIS DE VAUVENARGUES, *eighteenth-century French writer*

★ *The three great essentials to achieve anything worthwhile are first, hard work; second, stick-to-itiveness; and third, common sense.*
THOMAS EDISON, *twentieth-century American inventor*

★ *He started to sing as he tackled the thing that couldn't be done, and he did it.*
EDGAR GUEST, *twentieth-century American journalist and poet*

★ *Six essential qualities that are the key to success: sincerity, personal integrity, humility, courtesy, wisdom, charity.*
WILLIAM MENNINGER, *twentieth-century medical educator*

Upon the education of the people of this country the fate of this country depends.
BENJAMIN DISRAELI *nineteenth-century British politician and author*

No great achievement is possible without persistent work.
BERTRAND RUSSELL *twentieth-century English philosopher*

You know you will never get to the end of the journey. But this, so far from discouraging, only adds to the joy and glory of the climb.
SIR WINSTON CHURCHILL *twentieth-century British statesman*

BLUEPRINT FOR SUCCESS

Andrea Garney
American writer

1. Know yourself—well.
2. Prepare a plan of action—but always have a back-up.
3. Acknowledge that there is more than one way to achieve your dream—maybe even two or three.
4. Own your mistakes—and learn from them.
5. Recognize distractions—before they sink your ship.
6. Embrace change—it makes a much better friend than enemy.
7. Always move forward—nothing was ever accomplished by standing still.
8. Accept the reality of calculated risk—nothing ventured, nothing gained.
9. Prepare for a rainy day—sooner or later one will come.
10. Help and encourage others along the way—you'll be a better person for it.

Man was designed for accomplishment, engineered for success, and endowed with the seeds of greatness.

ZIG ZIGLAR
twentieth-century motivational speaker and author

Meet the Dream Weavers

I do not see myself as disabled.

Oscar Pistorius

Oscar Pistorius calls himself the fastest man on no legs! He is indeed one of the fastest men in the world. He hopes to prove it one day by competing in the Olympics.

Pistorius was born without fibulas, the long, thin outer bones that run between the ankles and the knees. When he was only eleven months old, doctors amputated his legs from the knee down. Pistorius has special prosthetics for running—the Cheetah® Flex-Foot provided by the runner's sponsor, Ossur. They are sophisticated, metal, J-shaped mechanisms that enable Pistorius to run.

The young sprinter from South Africa has always had a passion for competing athletically. He has played rugby and polo. He has competed in the Paralympics, winning many gold medals and breaking records in 100-, 200-, and 400-meter sprints. He has kept his own record nineteen times in one year and has often competed against able-bodied athletes.

Pistorius is a well-trained and hard-fighting athlete, and many believe he is deserving of the chance to compete in the Olympics. On May 16, 2008, the Court of Arbitration for Sport in Lausanne, Switzerland, ruled unanimously in favor of Pistorius. The twenty-one-year-old sprinter would be allowed to compete, as long as he qualified in August, in the Beijing Games 400-meter trials.

Critics of the decision to allow Pistorius to compete believe the Cheetah® Flex-Foot prosthetics give him an unfair advantage since they work as shock absorbers and so could keep the runner from tiring and may help him on curves and give him a longer stride. Yet, the prosthetics are not robotic. They attach to the natural knee and must be operated solely by the power of the runner's body. Unfortunatey, Pistorius failed to qualify in Beijing. He hopes to try again in London in 2012. However, in running at all, and in fighting for the right to participate in the Olympics against able-bodied runners, he exemplifies the spirit of the Olympians.

Whether or not Pistorius ever wins gold in the Olympics, he has won already. He has beaten the self-pity that could have ruled his life. He has fought for something he feels strongly about; and he has sent a message to disabled people everywhere that they, too, with determination and hard work, can beat the odds—they, too, can be winners!

Give diligence to make your calling and election sure:
for if ye do these things, ye shall never fall.
2 PETER 1:10 KJV

THE POWER OF POTENTIAL

Do you have a dream that you feel you have no hope of achieving? Ask God to help you plot a course to success, showing you effective paths around the obstacles that lie in your way.

What lies behind us and what lies before us are tiny matters compared to what lies within us.

RALPH WALDO EMERSON
nineteenth-century American essayist and poet

WISDOM SPEAKS

All my life so far, someone has been there to tell me what to do and when to do it—at least where the basic structure of my life was concerned. Now I'm entering a phase of my life where the choices are all up to me. What do I do now?

It is by his freedom that a person knows himself, by his sovereignty over his own life that a person measures himself.

ELIE WIESEL
twentieth-century American author and spokesman for Holocaust survivors

Freedom is not the right to do as you please; it is the liberty to do as you ought.

AUTHOR UNKNOWN

Knowledge comes, but wisdom lingers. It may not be difficult to store up in the mind a vast quantity of facts within a comparatively short time, but the ability to form judgments requires the severe discipline of hard work and the tempering heat of experience and maturity.

CALVIN COOLIDGE
thirtieth U.S. president

You've got to be brave, and you've got to be bold. Brave enough to take your chance on your own discriminations—what's right and what's wrong, what's good and what's bad.

ROBERT FROST
beloved twentieth-century American poet

I'm excited about my future, but there are so many question marks. How can I face the future when I have no idea what to expect?

Never be afraid to trust an unknown future to a known God.

CORRIE TEN BOOM
Dutch evangelist and Holocaust survivor

The future is God's: which means that, wherever the individual being goes, in life or death, God is there.

HANS KÜNG
twentieth-century German theologian

The only light upon the future is faith.

THEODOR HOECKER

God's plans like lilies, pure and white, unfold;
We must not tear the close-shut leaves apart;
Time will reveal the chalices of gold.

MAY LOUISE RILEY SMITH
twentieth-century American author and poet

I want to do so much, be so much, and succeed. Do you have any advice for me?

Be patient with everyone, but above all with yourself.

FRANCIS DE SALES
seventeenth-century bishop of Geneva and Roman Catholic saint

The person who succeeds is not the one who holds back, fearing failure, nor the one who never fails . . . but rather the one who moves on in spite of failure.

CHARLES R. SWINDOLL
twentieth-century author and theologian

A great many people go through life in bondage to success. They are in mortal dread of failure. I do not have to succeed. I have only to be true to the highest I know—success or failure are in the hands of God.

E. STANLEY JONES
twentieth-century Christian missionary and theologian

W I S D O M   S P E A K S

I'm so happy to be a graduate. It was a long and arduous road, but I made it. However, I'm worried about making mistakes in this important next phase of my life. What can I do to avoid mistakes and failures?

Mistakes are a part of life; you can't avoid them. All you can hope is that they won't be too expensive and that you don't make the same mistake twice.

LEE IACOCCA
twentieth-century businessman

Never let mistakes or wrong directions, of which every man falls into many, discourage you. There is precious instruction to be got by finding where we were wrong.

THOMAS CARLYLE
nineteenth-century Scottish essayist and historian

Sometimes a noble failure serves the world as faithfully as a distinguished success.

EDWARD DOWDEN
twentieth-century Irish literary critic and poet

If you have made mistakes . . . there is always another chance for you . . . you may have a fresh start any moment you choose, for this thing we call "failure" is not the falling down, but the staying down.

MARY PICKFORD
twentieth-century star of silent films

Fork in the Road

Sue Rhodes Dodd

My college major was general, and the job market was looking for seasoned specialists. I was caught in the common dilemma: prospective employers wanted me to have more experience, but I couldn't land a job to get the needed experience. It was discouraging to try and enter the work force only to encounter one detour after another.

So I accepted the first real offer that came along—as an office clerk. Most of my coworkers had never been to college, much less earned a bachelor's degree. My education didn't get me more income, and my supervisor was not impressed with my degree. College didn't help me at that job, and there really were no major career-advancement opportunities. But I didn't care; I had a paycheck and a job, and that's all I cared about.

Once I had a year's worth of work experience under my belt, I started the job-application process again, this time with renewed fervor and confidence. One of my first interviews was with a TV station with an office-clerk opening. After several interviews, I was sure an offer was forthcoming.

But when the manager called me, his news was disheartening. "If I hire you for the clerk position, it's just a question of time before you leave my department and go over to the news group," he said.

I was miffed, but he was right. The clerk job was indeed just a stepping stone. My communications-arts major made me a jack of several trades and a master of none. I had courses in TV, radio, film, print media, theatre, and debate. It was the perfect major for me—mostly because I really couldn't make up my mind which area I liked the best.

Within a couple of months of job hunting, I had not one, two, three, but *four* terrific opportunities. I had not been eliminated in the first review process. I was delighted: they were all considering me! One was with a training-film company, one with an advertising agency, one with a newspaper, and one with a radio station.

They all were appealing. All entry level. All required my degree. They all would be challenging and sounded like fun. I could see myself in any of the jobs.

I had no clue which one to accept. I talked with the three men in my life—my dad, my brother, and my husband. They thought each possibility held great opportunity for me. So I continued in the application and interviewing process for each job, hoping for the best.

I didn't know it then, but this fork in the road would have vastly different outcomes, depending on which communications industry I chose.

What I did know was to pray. "Lord, show me the right path," I said. "Give me Your favor and direction. Which way do I go with the rest of my life?"

Months dragged by. I called, wrote, interviewed, followed up, and kept checking on new possibilities. But mostly I waited.

Then came the offer from the newspaper. I've never been sorry. For me, it was the perfect match, though I hadn't put the puzzle pieces together yet.

When I was in sixth grade, I wrote a play. My school produced it, and I directed it and had a starring role. When I was in high school and college, I wrote some scripts for TV, radio, and film. Again, I enjoyed the process of producing and sometimes being in the productions. I was on the debate team in junior high. I worked for the high-school and college newspapers, had a radio show, and worked on a number of film crews.

But my senior year in college brought an epiphany. Instead of producing a TV show as most of the other students were doing, I did a research paper. I realized I loved it! I read and interviewed people, often gathering much more knowledge than was needed for the specific research thesis. I was curious and eager to find out more. Best of all, I liked assimilating a volume of information and writing about it.

For me, the persuasion of debate or advertising wasn't nearly as interesting as the research and the writing. The high of filming or taping a show wasn't nearly as exhilarating as the creative process behind the scenes. There was a common thread in all these experiences, and God was kind enough to direct my footsteps even when I was very unsure about which road at the fork best suited me.

The newspaper job when I was two years out of college committed me to a road that has been exciting and challenging. I've interviewed interesting people and written about joyful and tragic events. I've been published in newspapers, magazines, journals, manuals, and books. Nearly thirty years later, I'm still writing and loving every minute. Some side trips through corporate management, book editing, sales, and computer software testing have enhanced income, but I keep returning to my first love: writing.

God knew all along what I needed. He knew my heart's desire before I did. Even though it sometimes seemed that my route had no direction or was laden with potholes, the Lord was mapping my course. With Him in the driver's seat, the journey is always worth it.[2]

Dear Graduate,

You purposed in your heart to do what was at hand, and now you have reached a platform that none can take from you.

Celebrate your accomplishment not with foolish activities but in solitude. For then you will know the joy that comes from work well done.

Do not be discouraged by the numbness that descends on all major life events. You will realize the importance and beauty of what has taken place as it is reflected in your day-to-day life.

Enjoy the emotion now and the impact of your knowledge from this moment forward.

I am proud of you. I celebrate your accomplishment with you.

Sincerely,

Someone Who Loves You

Many good things come from what a man says. And the work of his hands rewards him.

PROVERBS 12:14 NIRV

Genius is 1 percent inspiration and 99 percent perspiration.

THOMAS EDISON
twentieth-century American inventor

Education is not the filling of a pail, but the lighting of a fire.

WILLIAM BUTLER YEATS
twentieth-century Irish poet and dramatist

SAY YES TO THOSE WHO HELPED YOU ALONG THE WAY

Remembering to Say "Thank You"

*Gratitude is the praise we offer God:
for teachers kind, benefactors never to be
forgotten, for all who have advantaged me,
by writings, sermons, converse, prayers, examples,
for all these and all others which I know,
which I know not, open, hidden,
remembered, and forgotten.*

LANCELOT ANDREWES
sixteenth-century Anglican clergyman

T H A N K   Y O U !

Thank those who helped you on your journey:

Your parents, for their love and care and years of saving to pay for your education

The teacher who gave you a passion for learning

The classmate who helped you believe in yourself

The professor who forced you to work harder

The classmate who challenged your opinions and caused you to review them

The instructor who drew out your gifts and talents

The school administrators who worked behind the scenes to give you the best education possible

In gratitude for your own good fortune, you must render in return some sacrifice of your life for another life.
ALBERT SCHWEITZER
twentieth-century theologian, philosopher, missionary physician, and music scholar

Thankfulness is a soil in which pride does not easily grow.
MICHAEL RAMSEY
twentieth-century archbishop of Canterbury

Gratitude is born in hearts that take time to count up past mercies.
CHARLES EDWARD JEFFERSON
twentieth-century Congregational minister

Have you thanked God for helping you with your . . . ?

☐ Classes   ☐ Grades

☐ Teachers   ☐ Curriculum

☐ Schoolwork   ☐ Friends

☐ Parents   ☐ Family

☐ Joy   ☐ Spiritual Growth

☐ Neighbors   ☐ Activities

☐ Success

Nothing is more honorable than a grateful heart.

SENECA

first-century Roman statesman, dramatist, and philosopher

Gratitude is the memory of the heart.

JEAN-BAPTISTE MASSIEU

eighteenth-century French monk and political activist

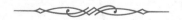

My heart leaps for joy and I will give thanks to him in song.

PSALM 28:7

Meet the Dream Weavers

Those who stand for nothing
fall for anything.

Alexander Hamilton

Tragedy shapes people in many ways. For some, it stifles their desire for a better life. But for others, it fuels a deep inner fire to triumph over the misfortunes of the past.

Alexander Hamilton overcame tragedy early in life, only to meet an early and equally tragic end. Nevertheless, he refused to allow his difficult childhood to serve as an excuse for not making a difference.

Born an illegitimate son in the British West Indies in 1757, Hamilton began his life with ridicule and disapproval. By the time Alexander was eleven years old, his father had abandoned his family and his mother had died of a "severe fever." His cousin adopted him but soon committed suicide, and once again Alexander Hamilton was orphaned. A local merchant then agreed to adopt him. When Alexander was fifteen years old, his adopted father raised the funds to send him to New England for better schooling.

At age nineteen, Alexander Hamilton joined a volunteer militia to fight the British. Quickly, Hamilton's character and abilities attracted the attention and deep confidence of George Washington, resulting in his appointment to serve as Washington's aide-de-camp.

After the conclusion of the Revolutionary War, he founded the Bank of New York. In 1787 he recruited John Jay and James Madison to join him in crafting a defense of the newly ratified Constitution. This compilation of eighty-five essays, of which he wrote fifty-one, is now known as the *Federalist Papers.* To this day, they serve as the primary source for interpreting the U.S. Constitution.

In 1789 President George Washington appointed him as the nation's first secretary of the treasury. During his tenure, he helped found the United States Mint, the first national bank, and the precursor to the Coast Guard.

Advocating a strong central government, Hamilton utilized his gift for building coalitions and formed the Federalist Party in 1792—the first U.S. political party. To further his views, he founded the present-day newspaper called the *New York Post* in 1801.

Tragically, Hamilton died as the result of a duel with Aaron Burr in 1804. But his many accomplishments can't be discounted. One might say that he shares his achievement with the local merchant who took the hand of an unfortunate orphan boy and put him on the path to greatness.

Thank God no matter what happens.
1 THESSALONIANS 5:18 MSG

THE POWER OF POTENTIAL

Even adults need personal heroes, someone to spur them on to great things. Do you have one? Look around you—it might be a parent, a grandparent, a family member, or family friend. Perhaps it is someone from your church. Find someone you admire, then watch and listen.

The crucible for silver and the furnace for gold, but the LORD tests the heart.
PROVERBS 17:3

ATTITUDE OF GRATITUDE

No one who achieves success does so without the help of others. The wise and confident acknowledge this help with gratitude.

ALFRED NORTH WHITEHEAD
eighteenth-century British mathematician, logician, and philosopher

We should all be thankful for those people who rekindle the inner spirit.

ALBERT SCHWEITZER
twentieth-century medical missionary, author, and winner of the Nobel Peace Prize

One can never pay in gratitude; one can only pay "in kind" somewhere else in life.

ANNE MORROW LINDBERGH
twentieth-century pioneering American aviator and author

The vocation of every man and woman is to serve other people.

LEO TOLSTOY
nineteenth-century Russian writer ranked among the greatest novelists in world literature

Do all the good you can,
By all the means you can,
In all the ways you can,
In all the places you can,
At all the times you can,
To all the people you can,
As long as ever you can.

JOHN WESLEY
eighteenth-century clergyman of the Church of England

STAYING CONNECTED

Everyone knows that after graduation people go off in different directions and time and distance take a toll on relationships. But that doesn't have to happen to you.

Consider these principles for staying connected:

★ Make plans for a specific date in the future to get together. It can't be "six months from now" or "let's get together soon." It needs to be a specific date with a specific place and time.

★ Learn the fine art of sending cards. In our electronic age this might sound cheesy, but nothing means more than a greeting you can hold in your hand. Next time you're at the card store, pick up several and buy some stamps to have on hand. No special occasion required.

★ Don't forget to gather those addresses, e-mail addresses, and phone numbers before everyone heads off for who knows where.

★ Make a point to tell your old friends about your new friends, and look for ways to introduce them.

★ Keep making memories. It's great to talk about the old days when you get together but even better to spend your time creating new memories.

Long Division

Alison Simpson

When I was in fifth grade, I had the privilege of being in Mrs. Francis's class. My older brother raved about her when he heard she would be my teacher. He, along with the rest of the school, loved her . . . thought she was the best teacher ever. She was fun, she was smart, and she was always one step ahead of her students. No one could get anything past her, but everyone still loved her and thought she was the coolest teacher in the school.

The memory of Mrs. Francis that I cherish the most (other than our class making Christmas cookies at her house one Saturday morning) was when I was struggling with long division. I hated long division, and I was *awful* at it. I'm not exaggerating about this. Math in general was way over my head. So when I encountered long division for the first time, I was filled with trepidation. And sure enough, my homework assignments revealed to Mrs. Francis that I was most definitely in need of help.

One afternoon after class, Mrs. Francis told me she was putting a note to my parents in my backpack. At first I was horrified. But then she explained that she wanted to help me, and she wanted permission to keep me after class. I reluctantly presented the note to my mom, and she agreed that from now on, I'd spend two days a week, after school, trying to master long division with Mrs. Francis.

And my fears were correct . . . it was frustrating and hard. I remember sitting in the front row of desks staring at the blackboard while she showed me how to work problems, and I felt clueless. Then she had me up at the blackboard, asking me to try, affirming my answers when they were right, and tenderly correcting them when they were wrong. Somehow, faced with a challenge I felt for sure I'd never master, she made me feel like I was smart. She helped me see that I could get this, with perseverance, patience, and a positive attitude.

Not only did she teach me long division, she also taught me that it was worth it to her to help me. *Why?* I wondered. She could have sent a note home to my parents, saying, "Alison is not grasping long division. Please work with her on this." But she didn't pass the buck. She decided that this was a perfect opportunity to help me see what I could do, and she knew she could help make it happen for me. She took me on as her responsibility because she cared enough about me not only as a student but also as a person.

Challenges are not opportunities for failure—they're invitations to grow. I learned that best when I was standing at the blackboard with Mrs. Francis. As hard as long division seemed to me, she taught me that it's possible for me to face my fear and then move on to bigger and better challenges. It's all part of being the best kind of "me" that I can be. Smaller challenges lead to bigger challenges, but the concept is the same: patience, a positive attitude, and perseverance are three "must-haves" in your toolbox for life. If you've got those things ready and available to you, you can tackle just about anything that comes your way in life.

When I graduated from high school, I moved away and lost touch with Mrs. Francis. But she was definitely my favorite teacher because she cared—not just with her words, but with her actions and her investment in my life. It reminds me of the old adage that children learn how to live, not from our words alone, but from the way we live our lives.

As you seek out the right direction for yourself, I challenge you to find ways of making investments that really make a difference in the lives of others. If you want to make your mark upon the world, that's a terrific place to start. And as you take on challenges that seem fierce, remember to always have the right tools . . . and remember to offer all your challenges to God so He can reveal His strength in your weaknesses.

And you never know, He might even put someone like Mrs. Francis in your path to remind you that, yes, you *can* do the thing you fear the most. And when you've done that, you might even find yourself in the privileged position of being a "Mrs. Francis" to someone else, and watching that beautiful transformation—fear turned into confidence and strength.[3]

THE POWER OF POTENTIAL

Who in your life has helped you face a challenge? If you were to write her a thank-you note, what would you say?

Always be thankful.
COLOSSIANS 3:15 NLT

*Make it a habit to tell people thank you—to express
your appreciation, sincerely and without the expectation
of anything in return. Truly appreciate those around
you, and you'll soon find many others around you. Truly
appreciate life, and you'll find that you have more of it.*
RALPH MARSTON
writer of inspirational quotations

*To speak gratitude is courteous and pleasant,
to enact gratitude is generous and noble,
but to live gratitude is to touch Heaven.*
JOHANNES A. GAERTNE

What I Could

LOUIS PASTEUR
nineteenth-century French theoretical scientist

Say to yourselves first, "What have I done for my
instruction?" and as you gradually advance, "What have
I done for my country?" until the time comes when you
may have the immense happiness of thinking that you have
contributed in some way to the progress and to the good of
humanity. But whether our efforts are, or not, favored by life,
let us be able to say, when we come near to the great goal,
"I have done what I could."

SAY YES TO YOUR PASSIONS AND GIFTS

Finding Out What
Makes You Unique

*Success means we go to sleep at night
knowing that our talents and abilities were
used in a way that served others.*
MARIANNE WILLIAMSON
co-leader of the U.S. Department of Peace Movement

*Nothing great was ever achieved
without enthusiasm.*
RALPH WALDO EMERSON
nineteenth-century American essayist and poet

The Slightest Effort

Orison Swett Marden
Founder of Success *magazine*

A lobster, when left high and dry among the rock, has no instinct or energy enough to work his way back to the sea, but waits for the sea to come to him. If it does not come, he remains where he is and dies, although the slightest effort would enable him to reach the waves, which are perhaps within a yard of him.

The world is full of human lobsters; men stranded on the rocks of indecision and procrastination, who, instead of putting forth their own energies, are waiting for some grand billow of good fortune to set them afloat.

Rebellion against your handicaps gets you nowhere. Self-pity gets you nowhere. One must have the adventurous daring to accept oneself as a bundle of possibilities and undertake the most interesting game in the world—making the most of one's best.

HARRY EMERSON FOSDICK
twentieth-century Protestant preacher, professor, and author

Be still when you have nothing to say; when genuine passion moves you, say what you've got to say, and say it hot.

D. H. LAWRENCE
twentieth-century English novelist

Our great object in time is not to waste our passions and gifts on the things external that we must leave behind, but that we cultivate within us all that we can carry into the eternal progress beyond.

EDWARD BULWER-LYTTON
nineteenth-century English novelist, poet, playwright, and politician

I have walked with people whose eyes are full of light but who see nothing in sea or sky, nothing in city streets, nothing in books. It was far better to sail forever in the night of blindness with sense, and feeling, and mind, than to be content with the mere act of seeing.

HELEN KELLER
twentieth-century American deafblind lecturer and author

THE POWER OF POTENTIAL

Laughter has been known to inspire love, and love, laughter. Laugh long and often with those you love. Your life and the lives of all those around you will be better for it. How can you add a good laugh to your day today?

Dream no small dreams for they have no power to move the hearts of men.

JOHANN WOLFGANG VON GOETHE
nineteenth-century German poet, novelist, and playwright

A day without laughter is a day wasted.

CHARLIE CHAPLIN
twentieth-century actor and comedian

[God] will yet fill your mouth with laughter and your lips with shouts of joy.

Job 8:21

31

Meet the Dream Weavers

I . . . indeed want to set religion back—not just a hundred years but nineteen hundred years, to the Book of Acts, when first-century followers of Christ were accused of turning the Roman Empire upside down.

Billy Graham

"The world has yet to see what God can do with a man fully consecrated to him," evangelist D. L. Moody once challenged. Many believe that in the life of the Reverend Billy Graham, that challenge has been met. Few people have left an imprint on the world for the cause of Christ more than Billy Graham. And few people have seemingly consecrated themselves to Christ and the gospel like he has.

Born on November 7, 1918, and raised on a dairy farm in Charlotte, North Carolina, Billy Graham dedicated his life to Jesus at age sixteen after listening to evangelist Mordecai Ham during a series of revival meetings.

After graduating from college, Graham pastored a church for a short time before joining Youth for Christ (YFC), an evangelistic ministry to youth and military servicemen and women. His experience with YFC helped him discover he had a passion and a gift for preaching. It also fueled a fire deep in his bones for sharing the gospel in open-air meetings.

In 1949 Graham scheduled his first high-profile crusade in Los Angeles. Many believe William Randolph Hearst, the publishing mogul, ordered his newspapers to "puff Graham" by promoting the meetings. Although scheduled for three weeks, the meetings lasted more than eight, with overflow crowds totaling approximately 350,000 people. Almost overnight, Billy Graham became America's most well-known evangelist.

Since then, Graham has preached to nearly 215 million people in more than 185 countries and territories. In fact, Reverend Graham has preached the gospel to more people in person than anyone else in history. Hundreds of millions more have been reached through television, radio, and film.

During the Cold War, Graham was the first notable evangelist to preach behind the Iron Curtain, attracting large crowds in the Soviet Union and Eastern Europe. Later, he appeared in China and North Korea.

In the turbulent 1960s, Billy Graham chose the path of most resistance, refusing to speak to segregated groups, one time tearing down the ropes that separated whites from blacks. "There is no scriptural basis for segregation. . . . The ground at the foot of the cross is level, and it touches my heart when I see whites standing shoulder to shoulder with blacks at the cross," he once commented.

He paid the bail money to release Dr. Martin Luther King Jr. from jail and invited him to share the pulpit with him at a crusade in New York City. During that sixteen-week revival, 2.3 million listeners heard him at Madison Square Garden, Yankee Stadium, and Times Square. Through the experience, Graham and King became friends.

While taking a hard stance toward racism, Graham refused to take sides in political battles. Ironically, Graham has served as a spiritual advisor to every U.S. president since Eisenhower. He has also regularly appeared on the Gallup Poll's "Ten Most Admired Men in the World" and was ranked seventh on Gallup's list of admired people for the twentieth century. Throughout the course of his ministry, he has authored twenty-six books, which have been translated into several languages.

Best of all, Reverend Graham has avoided many of the pitfalls that have caused other notable Christian celebrities to stumble. While traveling, he took great precautions to ensure he didn't place himself in potentially compromising situations with the opposite sex. He refused to receive an excessive salary, refused to criticize local churches, and avoided giving exaggerated numbers when reporting on his campaigns.

When people dedicate their gifts and passions and consecrate their hearts to Christ, anything can happen.

A gift opens the way for the giver and ushers him into the presence of the great.

PROVERBS 18:16

THE POWER OF POTENTIAL

What are your gifts and talents? Consider your:
  Goals
  Hobbies
  Favorite subjects
  Most-read books
  Friends, and what you like to do with them
  Parents, and where they feel you excel
  Time, and what you do with it
Most importantly, listen to your heart, your passion from within. Do one thing today that will help you better enjoy the person God created you to be.

You have granted him the desire of his heart and have not withheld the request of his lips.
PSALM 21:2

The future belongs to those who believe in the beauty of their dreams.
ELEANOR ROOSEVELT
one of the most active first ladies in American history

We have different gifts, according to the grace given us. If a man's gift is prophesying, let him use it in proportion to his faith. If it is serving, let him serve; if it is teaching, let him teach; if it is encouraging, let him encourage; if it is contributing to the needs of others, let him give generously; if it is leadership, let him govern diligently; if it is showing mercy, let him do it cheerfully.

ROMANS 12:6–8

There are different kinds of gifts, but the same Spirit. There are different kinds of service, but the same Lord. There are different kinds of working, but the same God works all of them in all men. Now to each one the manifestation of the Spirit is given for the common good. To one there is given through the Spirit the message of wisdom, to another the message of knowledge by means of the same Spirit, to another faith by the same Spirit, to another gifts of healing by that one Spirit, to another miraculous powers, to another prophecy, to another distinguishing between spirits, to another speaking in different kinds of tongues, and to still another the interpretation of tongues. All these are the work of one and the same Spirit, and he gives them to each one, just as he determines.

1 CORINTHIANS 12:4–11

I thank God for my handicaps, for, through them, I have found myself, my work, and my God.

HELEN KELLER
twentieth-century American deafblind lecturer and author

Whatever you do, work at it with all your heart, as working for the Lord.

COLOSSIANS 3:23

Dost thou love life? Then do not squander time, for that is the stuff life is made of.

BENJAMIN FRANKLIN
eighteenth-century American statesman and philosopher

Meet the Dream Weavers

Christianity, if false, is of no importance,
and if true, of infinite importance. The only
thing it cannot be is moderately important.

C.S. Lewis

In the halls of academia, many scholars take a dim view of professing Christians. Adhering to the Christian faith requires belief in something people can't see, something that can't be scientifically verified.

C. S. Lewis, however, knew God had given him the ability to think as well as a keen imagination that enabled him to explore his faith and defend it against the onslaught of skeptics.

Clive Staples Lewis was born in Belfast, Ireland (now Northern Ireland), in 1898. Growing up, he attended boarding school in England and later graduated from Oxford University. He spent the rest of his life teaching English at Oxford and later at Cambridge.

Over the objections of his colleagues, Lewis began writing children's books, including his most well-known book, *The Lion, the Witch and the Wardrobe.* His Chronicles of Narnia series has sold over 100 million books.

But also close to his heart was the defense of the Christian faith. His books—especially *Mere Christianity*—answered the hardest questions of many skeptics and continue to do so today. Lewis's impeccable credentials, passion for his faith, and communication abilities enabled him to present a credible claim for the faith. But he also exhibited the courage to live his faith openly in the halls of academia. For that, we can all be grateful.

When the dream in your heart is one that God has planted there, a strange happiness flows into you. At that moment all of the spiritual resources of the universe are released to help you. Your praying is then at one with the will of God and becomes a channel for the Creator's always joyous, triumphant purposes for you and your world.

CATHERINE MARSHALL
greatly loved twentieth-century American author

THE POWER OF POTENTIAL

List the dreams you have about your future. Ask God to show you a pattern and direct you to His dream for your future.

_____

_____

_____

_____

_____

_____

_____

_____

_____

_____

_____

Be sure to use the abilities God has given you. . . . Put these abilities to work; throw yourself into your tasks . . .
1 TIMOTHY 4:14–15 TLB

God's gifts put man's best dreams to shame.
ELIZABETH BARRETT BROWNING
most famous poet of nineteenth-century Victorian England

Each man has his own gift from God; one has this gift, another has that.
1 CORINTHIANS 7:7

YOU Write the Songs

Bonnie Compton Hanson

"Mom!" Jay cried as he flew inside. "The eighth grade's having a talent contest. I want to enter! You know I love to sing. Maybe I can win some friends this way."

My smile stayed bright, but inside I sighed. Ever since we moved to this new town, Jay seemed to be a misfit. The other kids were richer, bolder, taller, more sophisticated—all one big clique. Even Jay's teachers appeared united against him.

Compared with them, Jay was the odd man out. With his growth spurt still in the future, a childish cherubic face, very shy manner, and obviously poor parents, he was way out of step with his classmates. But he did have a marvelous high voice, still unchanged.

"That's great!" I pretended. "What do you want to sing?"

"'I Write the Songs.' Because I love Barry Manilow. He sings and plays the piano both. I want to write songs, too, just like he does, when I grow up. Look, could you practice with me?"

"Are you sure you don't want to use a CD or tape instead?"

His eyes shone. "No, I'd much rather have you play for me. We'll be a team."

So we practiced. And practiced. And soon he sang it so well it brought tears to my eyes.

Wait till the contest night! He'd "knock 'em dead"—and break down those puzzling walls of prejudice on his middle-school campus.

The school auditorium was packed that night. As each performer sang, played, danced, or recited, large cheering sections rang out. Even though the performers were unpolished, the student team at the soundboard, under a teacher's supervision, made them sound professional. I could hardly wait for Jay's turn.

Finally they called his number. Sitting down to the piano, I joyfully played his introduction. Then he sang the first note.

Suddenly a horrendous electronic squeal poured out of the amplifiers. Laughter broke out both from the soundboard operators and their in-on-the-joke teacher.

Startled, Jay faltered and looked at the judges for advice or help. "Keep right on singing or you lose your turn," one snapped back. "No exceptions."

So he sang, even though not one of his awesome notes could be heard above the din of the amps "gain." Not one parent or teacher called a halt to the shrill back-curtain guffaws that quickly spread across the audience. No one applauded my son's heroic effort. Instead, some kids yelled out, "Loser!" Then others took up the chorus. Even the judges were grinning at each other.

White as a sheet, Jay bowed and left the stage, as the next contestant took the mike. Just like that, the amplifier "problems" miraculously disappeared. His humiliation was complete.

I've never felt so helpless. I could think of nothing to do or say to ease the anguish of my half-grown son.

I could hardly get him back to school the next day. The only thing that kept him going during those long hours of ridicule that day was knowing he did his best.

I wish I could say that the rest of the year was better. But it wasn't. Yet each morning he went back to school, and each evening he did his homework. He prayed and asked God for His help. He practiced. And he never gave up his dream of singing.

Then came high school. By the time he was a sophomore, ten inches taller, with a new deeper voice, and a new school, Jay blossomed. With his great voice and good looks, he soon had the lead in all the school musicals. He even became accompanist for his high-school choral groups, leading them to top honors in state contests. Later he returned to his school as part of the music staff.

Today as a grown man, Jay continues to lead musical groups, sing, perform, and compose music. Everyone who hears him is touched and thrilled. So is he.

Maybe you, too, have been ridiculed or put down or told to give up on your dreams. Maybe your junior-high or high-school days have sad memories that haunt you.

But, guess what? YOU "write the songs" in your life! YOU and God together are in charge of your dreams. No money for college? Do as millions of young people do—take a job and attend college online or nights or weekends—and meet some great new friends.

Seek counselors. Ask God's help. Find friends who believe in you. Seek God's will for your life. And believe in yourself.

That's what has enabled Jay to truly "write his own songs" in life. And to sing them with joy. And you can too![4]

No pessimist ever discovered the secrets of the stars,
or sailed to an uncharted land,
or opened a new heaven to the human spirit.
HELEN KELLER
twentieth-century American deafblind lecturer and author

THE POWER OF POTENTIAL

Do you have obstacles standing between you and your dreams? Have you tried and failed? Never give up! Seek God's will for your life. Then write your goals and your commitment to persevere.

Do not go where the path may lead; go instead where there is no path and leave a trail.

RALPH WALDO EMERSON
nineteenth-century American essayist and poet

Great works are performed not by strength but by perseverance.

SAMUEL JOHNSON
greatest English writer of the eighteenth century

Far away there in the sunshine are my highest aspirations.
I may not reach them, but I can look up and see their beauty,
believe in them, and try to follow where they lead.

LOUISA MAY ALCOTT
nineteenth-century American author

Andrew E. Durham

known as the Will Rogers of Indiana
Letter to his daughter Margaret on
September 3, 1942

Dear Margaret:

I was sorry to hear you hadn't made the grade and didn't get what you want[ed], but I would have been much sorrier if you hadn't tried. That's what gets me—this not trying. And while you may be quite a bit disappointed, you tried all the same, and that is the thing that counts much, much more.

Of all things, I never thought I would have a daughter in the Army or Navy, but now that things have happened as they have, and women are going into the War, why, I'm getting used to most anything. If I were you, and I wanted in, I'd keep pecking away until I got in. You said something about them wanting you to try for something like a job as a "private" in the Army. I am rather inclined to think you did right in not accepting that offer. You have an education, and better still, you have an ability that should rate you better than that of a private. It is true all of us can't be "Generals," but with your ability, your common sense, and a world of other good qualities, you, if you want to, and will stick with it, will be able to get in WAVE, or whatever it is, from some other state—Indiana, for instance.

There is a lot of bologna in this War, like all others, and I am told on good authority that it takes a political set-up to get the best. Honestly, when I heard you were trying Pennsylvania, I rather thought you would not be in the running. It just don't make sense for an Indiana girl to get a job like you wanted in the face of women (natives) in the second most populous State in the Union. Now above all things, don't repeat what I have said, and by no means give such as an excuse for missing the boat at Philadelphia, just keep mum, keep your own counsel, profit by your experience, and keep on trying in every way you can. If I get a chance I'll get to Indianapolis and try to learn what WAVE is doing in Indiana, if anything. I have been so busy, I haven't had time to go anyplace or do anything except keep the farms going, which is a big job.

Let me hear from you,

Pap

I'll Try and I Can't

Author Unknown

The little boy who says, "I'll try,"
Will climb to the hilltop.
The little boy who says "I can't,"
Will at the bottom stop.

"I'll try," does great things every day;
"I can't" gets nothing done;
Be sure then that you say, "I'll try,"
And let "I can't" alone.

WISDOM SPEAKS

I know that my goals will take time and patience. But how do I avoid discouragement as I face setbacks?

Don't judge each day by the harvest you reap but by the seeds that you plant.

ROBERT LOUIS STEVENSON
nineteenth-century Scottish novelist

Boast not of what thou would'st have done, but do what then thou would'st.

JOHN MILTON
seventeenth-century English poet and political writer

Trust your instinct to the end, though you can render no reason.

RALPH WALDO EMERSON
nineteenth-century American essayist and poet

A business that makes nothing but money is a poor business.

HENRY FORD
twentieth-century innovator and manufacturer of American cars

I would rather be beaten in the right than succeed in the wrong.

JAMES A. GARFIELD
twentieth U.S. president

Always bear in mind that your own resolution to success is more important than any other one thing.

ABRAHAM LINCOLN
sixteenth U.S. president

You Mustn't Quit!

Author Unknown

When things go wrong, as they sometimes will,
When the road you're trudging seems all uphill,
When the funds are low and the debts are high
And you want to smile, but you have to sigh,
When care is pressing you down a bit,
Rest! if you must—but never quit.

Life is queer, with its twists and turns,
As every one of us sometimes learns,
And many a failure turns about
When he might have won if he'd stuck it out;
Stick to your task, though the pace seems slow—
You may succeed with one more blow.

Success is failure turned inside out—
The silver tint of the clouds of doubt—
And you never can tell how close you are,
It may be near when it seems afar;
So stick to the fight when you're hardest hit—
It's when things seem worst that YOU MUSTN'T QUIT.

From a 1910 Speech Given in Paris at the Sorbonne

Theodore Roosevelt
twenty-sixth U.S. president

It is not the critic who counts, not the man who points out how the strong man stumbled, or where the doer of deeds could have done better. The credit belongs to the man who is actually in the arena, whose face is marred by dust and sweat and blood, who strives valiantly, who errs and comes short again and again, who knows the great enthusiasms, the great devotions, and spends himself in a worthy cause, who at best knows achievement and who at the worst if he fails at least fails while daring greatly so that his place shall never be with those cold and timid souls who know neither victory nor defeat.

Only if you reach the boundary will the boundary recede before you. And if you don't, if you confine your efforts, the boundary will shrink to accommodate itself to your efforts. And you can only expand your capacities by working to the very limit.
HUGH NIBLEY
twentieth-century writer and scholar

Ever since we first heard about you we have kept on praying and asking God to help you understand what he wants you to do; asking him to make you wise about spiritual things; and asking that the way you live will always please the Lord and honor him, so that you will always be doing good, kind things for others, while all the time you are learning to know God better and better.

Colossians 1:9–10 TLB

Brave and patriotic men are better than gold.
ABRAHAM LINCOLN
sixteenth U.S. president

Greatness

Zane Grey
twentieth-century American novelist

To bear up under loss;
To fight with bitterness of defeat and the weakness of grief;
To be victor over anger;
To smile when tears are close;
To resist disease and evil men and base instincts;
To hate hate and to love love;
To go on when it would seem good to die;
To look up with unquenchable faith
in something ever more about to be.
That is what any man can do, and be great.

Let not the foundation of our hope rest upon man's wisdom . . . but . . . God and His overruling providence.

FRANKLIN PIERCE
fourteenth U.S. president

If God had wanted me otherwise, He would have created me otherwise.

JOHANN WOLFGANG VON GOETHE
nineteenth-century German poet, novelist, and playwright

Energy will do anything that can be done in this world.

JOHANN WOLFGANG VON GOETHE
nineteenth-century German poet, novelist, and playwright

Energy and persistence conquer all things.

BENJAMIN FRANKLIN
eighteenth-century American statesman and philosopher

Hold Fast Your Dreams

Louise Driscoll
American poet

Hold fast your dreams!
Within your heart
Keep one still, secret spot
Where dreams may go,
And, sheltered so,
May thrive and grow
Where doubt and fear are not.
O keep a place apart,
Within your heart,
For little dreams to go!

In activity we must find our joy as well as glory; and labor, like everything else that is good, is its own reward.
EDWIN PERCY WHIPPLE
nineteenth-century essayist and critic

Go confidently in the direction of your dream. Live the life you have imagined.
HENRY DAVID THOREAU
nineteenth-century American writer, naturalist, and philosopher

Let us run with endurance the race that is set before us, looking unto Jesus, the author and finisher of our faith.
HEBREWS 12:1–2 NKJV

Doing is the great thing. For if, resolutely, people do what is right, in time they come to like doing it.
JOHN RUSKIN
most influential English critic of the 1800s

THE POWER OF POTENTIAL

Have you been tempted to give up on your dreams? Who helps you stay focused on your goals? Where can you look for encouragement? Write your own words of encouragement to yourself that you can return to when times get tough.

. . . we also glory in tribulations, knowing that tribulation produces perseverance; and perseverance, character; and character, hope. Now hope does not disappoint, because the love of God has been poured out in our hearts by the Holy Spirit who was given to us.

ROMANS 5:3–5 NKJV

Meet the Dream Weavers

I repent of ever having recorded one single song and ever having performed one concert if my music, and more importantly—my life—has not provoked you into godly jealousy, or to sell out more completely to Jesus!

Keith Green

What is your deepest desire? To build a successful career in business? To start a family? Our desires—which become apparent by our actions—betray our hearts. But what does God *want* our desire to be?

Born in New York but raised in California, Keith Green grew up in a family of musicians and was groomed for greatness. A young musical prodigy heralded in *Time* magazine, Green appeared on television talk shows and game shows, in commercials, and on television pilots. At age eleven he signed a recording contract with Decca Records, singing his own songs. But his career came to a halt when his competitor Donny Osmond stole the hearts of young girls across the country.

Although he came from a Jewish background, Keith Green grew up reading the New Testament—an "odd combination" that left him open-minded but deeply unsatisfied. After he had indulged in drugs, Asian mysticism, and "free love" like many other teenagers of his day, he met Melody, who became a believer, and the two married at the end of 1973. God "broke through [his] calloused heart," and Keith gave his life to Christ in 1975, after which he couldn't contain himself. He and Melody opened their home to prostitutes, drug addicts, and the homeless, much to the dismay of their neighbors. And as a result of living with the Greens, the houseguests were introduced to Jesus. This inspired Keith and Melody to form Last Days Ministries.

The next year, Green signed a contract with Sparrow Records, which led to five record albums including *No Compromise*. In 1979 he negotiated a release from his contract with Sparrow and released *So You Wanna Go Back to Egypt,* featuring a guest appearance by Bob Dylan. Green refused to charge people for the album or tickets to his concerts, only asking people to pay what they could afford.

About that same time Keith Green began distributing the Last Days Newsletter, which challenged Christians to share their faith and live without compromise. At its peak, over 300,000 readers received this publication.

Sharing Jesus with people who had never met him was Keith Green's desire, his passion. He wanted people to completely sell out their lives to Jesus. He once wrote:

> If your heart takes more pleasure in reading novels, or watching TV, or going to the movies, or talking to friends, rather than just sitting alone with God and embracing Him, sharing His cares and His burdens, weeping and rejoicing with Him, then how are you going to handle forever and ever in His presence? You'd be bored to tears in heaven, if you're not ecstatic about God now!

Perhaps his popularity could be attributed to the fact that Keith wrote songs reflecting his own spiritual struggles. When he sang about hypocrisy, he knew he was singing about himself as well. Before his music convicted others, it convicted him. His vulnerability connected him with his listeners and established a deep level of credibility.

On July 28, 1982, Keith Green died in an airplane accident along with his three-year-old son, Josiah, and his two-year-old daughter, Bethany. Melody was home with their one-year-old, Rebekah, while six weeks pregnant with their fourth child, Rachel. Keith was only twenty-eight years old.

In only seven years of knowing Jesus, Keith Green recorded five albums while having an impact upon not only his world, but *the* world, for the cause of Christ. Last Days Ministries sent out dozens of young people to the mission field, and countless others still listen to his music. By the end of his life, his childhood dream of becoming wealthy and famous had changed. Although controversial and, at times, misunderstood, Keith Green's passionate desire to share the gospel made a difference in his life.

> *Trust in the LORD with all your heart and lean not on your own understanding; in all your ways acknowledge him, and he will make your paths straight.*
>
> PROVERBS 3:5–6

THE POWER OF POTENTIAL

Are you ecstatic about God? Take time to be in His presence, ask Him to touch your heart, and discover His plan for you.

I can do everything through him who gives me strength.

PHILIPPIANS 4:13

Endurance is nobler than strength, and patience than beauty.

JOHN RUSKIN
most influential English critic of the 1800s

When we see ourselves in a situation, which must be endured and gone through, it is best to make up our minds to meet it with firmness, and accommodate everything to it in the best way practical.

THOMAS JEFFERSON
third U.S. president

Fired by Design

Rebekah Montgomery

Vic discovered that when a person is seeking God's direction, life sometimes takes surprising turns.

On a late spring afternoon in Findlay, Ohio, as he was driving his Pontiac to the pizza place where he worked, Vic recommitted himself to serving God. "Your will be done with my life," Vic remembers praying, never dreaming that God would take him at his word. Within the next several minutes, God rearranged his entire future.

As a student working his way through college, Vic had been making pizzas for about nine months. While he didn't intend to make a career of it, he had been giving it his best effort. However, on that afternoon, the assistant manager met him at the door to inform him of a change in his employment status.

"You're fired!"

"I was startled," Vic remembers, "but a thrill surged through me as I remembered the commitment I had just made. I was sure this was the hand of God working."

Badly in need of a paycheck, Vic took a job as an orderly at Blanchard Valley Hospital. However, his occupation was about to change again: Because of his college training, in addition to his orderly duties, Vic was sent to the lab to do emergency tests. Over test tubes and microscopes, he became acquainted with the hospital pathologist who needed someone to assist him with autopsies. He tapped Vic for the job. Vic showed such aptitude that he was placed on call for all of the autopsies in the county and the hospital.

Sometime later, Vic decided to apply to medical school.

He knew admissions standards were rigorous. Nervously, he interviewed with the acceptance committee on Friday. When he returned to school on Sunday afternoon, there was a letter in his mailbox. The pathologist with whom Vic worked at the hospital was also on the staff of the Ohio State Medical School. He had given Vic a glowing recommendation that helped cinch his admittance.

"Is getting fired a miracle?" asks Vic.

It is when God is leading. Vic has now been a surgeon for more than thirty years and has served as a medical missionary in various parts of the world for more than fifteen years.[5]

Consider it pure joy . . . whenever you face trials of many kinds, because you know that the testing of your faith develops perseverance.

JAMES 1:2–3

On Success

James A. Garfield
twentieth U.S. president

In order to have any success in life, or any worthy success, you must resolve to carry into your work a fullness of knowledge—not merely a sufficiency, but more than a sufficiency. Be fit for more than the thing you are now doing. Let everyone know that you have a reserve in yourself; that you have more power than you are now using. If you are not too large for the place you occupy, you are too small for it.

THE POWER OF POTENTIAL

Always be willing and eager to do beyond what is necessary to fulfill your obligations. List two tasks you are working on and how you can complete them—beyond expectations.

If passion drives you, let reason hold the reins.

BENJAMIN FRANKLIN
eighteenth-century American statesman and philosopher

Three Words of Strength

Friedrich von Schiller
German poet, philosopher, and historian

There are three lessons I would write,
Three words, as with a burning pen,
In tracings of eternal light,
Upon the hearts of men.

Have Hope. Through clouds environ round,
And gladness hides her face in scorn,
Put off the shadow from thy brow:
No night but hath its morn.

Have Faith. Where'er thy bark is driven—
The calm's disport, the tempest's mirth—
Know this: God rules the hosts of heaven,
The inhabitants of earth.

Have Love. Not love alone for one,
But man, as man, thy brother call;
And scatter, like a circling sun,
Thy charities on all.

Whatever course you decide upon, there is always someone to tell you that you are wrong. There are always difficulties arising, which tempt you to believe that your critics are right. To map out a course of action and follow it to an end requires . . . courage.

RALPH WALDO EMERSON
nineteenth-century American essayist and poet

Nothing is particularly hard if you divide it into small jobs.

HENRY FORD
twentieth-century innovator and manufacturer of American cars

If you only keep adding little by little, it will soon become a big heap.

HESIOD
seventh-century B.C. Greek poet

You may have to fight a battle more than once to win it.

MARGARET THATCHER
British prime minister, 1979– 1990

Hold fast to dreams, for if dreams die, life is like a broken winged bird that cannot fly.

ROBERT FROST
beloved twentieth-century American poet

Success is going from failure to failure without loss of enthusiasm.

SIR WINSTON CHURCHILL
twentieth-century British statesman

The Race

In a race, everyone runs but only one person gets first prize. So run your race to win. To win the contest you must deny yourselves many things that would keep you from doing your best. An athlete goes to all this trouble just to win a blue ribbon or a silver cup, but we do it for a heavenly reward that never disappears. So I run straight to the goal with purpose in every step. I fight to win. I'm not just shadow-boxing or playing around. Like an athlete I punish my body, treating it roughly, training it to do what it should, not what it wants to. Otherwise I fear that after enlisting others for the race, I myself might be declared unfit and ordered to stand aside.

1 CORINTHIANS 9:24–27 TLB

THE POWER OF POTENTIAL

Are you willing to count the cost and follow through until your dream is realized? Write down the sacrifices and commitments you know you will have to make, along with your decision to make them.

IDENTIFY YOUR DREAMS

FIVE PRACTICAL STEPS

1. Find a quiet place, and go there often to think and pray.

2. Ask God to clear your mind, and note those things that your thoughts turn to as you relax.

3. Meditate on those that burn brightly inside your heart. There may be no more than one.

4. Write them down.

5. Ask God to help you prioritize your list.

The future is too interesting and dangerous to be entrusted to any predictable, reliable agency. We need all the fallibility we can get.

LEWIS THOMAS
twentieth-century physician, writer, and educator

P U R S U E   Y O U R   D R E A M S

T E N   P R A C T I C A L   S T E P S

1. **Pray:** ask God to help you as you pursue your dream. Make Him your closest ally.

2. **Strategize:** sit down with paper and pen and think about what you can do in the next three months to move closer to your dream.

3. **Commit:** resolve to stay with the plan, and avoid distractions.

4. **Secure:** think about where you can obtain help— people, institutions, further education, etc.

5. **Act:** take the first step.

6. **Track:** record your progress from day to day.

7. **Relax:** don't become overwhelmed or impatient. It will all come together in time.

8. **Celebrate:** encourage yourself by reflecting on your past successes.

9. **Reenlist:** after the first three months, evaluate your progress and move on to the next three months.

10. **Walk:** your dream will probably be realized in small, but increasing, increments rather than one big explosion of success. Walk out your dream—one day at a time.

From the glow of enthusiasm,
I let the melody escape. I pursue it.
Breathless I catch up with it.
It flies again, it disappears,
it plunges into a chaos of diverse emotions.
I catch it again, I seize it,
I embrace it with delight . . . I multiply it
by modulations, and at last I triumph
in the first theme. There is the
whole symphony.

LUDWIG VAN BEETHOVEN
nineteenth-century German composer
and pianist, possibly the greatest of all time

Our truest life is when we are
in dreams awake.
HENRY DAVID THOREAU
nineteenth-century American writer,
naturalist, and philosopher

Say Cheese

Kimberly J. Fish

Kali Cavanaugh patted Queenie's brown hindquarters as the goat climbed up the shallow steps and through the window frame following a short line of other milking goats ambling toward the pasture. Dusting her hands, Kali leaned through the sill reaching for the glass-paned window, but her nose caught scents of rosemary and lemongrass weaving through the currents in the air. As Joaquin poured Queenie's gallon and a half offering into the pasteurizer, Kali walked around the milking station, ducking her head under the large wooden beam dividing the pre- and post-Spanish American War sections of her rambling barn.

She saw her sister ladling yesterday's curds into the cylinder molds Kali had bought from a retiring Provençal farmer on her last trip to the "old country." Although, truth be told, it wasn't her old country, it was her aunt's. But since she'd been raised by the woman with a lilting French accent, she'd adopted "ze leetle corner of heaven" as her own.

"Okay, Lacy, want to tell me what you're doing getting *your* hands dirty?" Kali looked at her sister's blouse and tailored jeans. "You once told me going behind the manufacturing door was not in the job description."

"Well that was before I found out working for you included wearing four different hats. The only time I get to have any fun throwing around my executive clout is when you need me to schmooze clients." Lacy removed her apron, looping it over Kali's shoulders instead.

Kali took the ladle from her sister's inept hands and measured even spoonfuls into the molds. "Yes, but you do it so well."

Lacy wiped her hands on a terry cloth. "But I just graduated from college. I should be doing something more in line with my expensive bachelor's degree. There's bound to be a high-rise, corner office needing my skills. Don't you think?"

Kali smiled into her sister's familiar blue eyes. "It's a good thing I employed you as my business manager before Chicago or New York lured you away. Do you remember how I planned on being a corporate attorney in D.C.? Well, look at me now, elbow-deep in goat-milk product. Progress isn't always pretty."

"I appreciate what you're doing here for the gourmet food industry," Lacy said with some disdain, "but it would appear your brain has been curdled by all this . . . cheese."

"Because I'm not practicing law?"

Lacy folded her arms across her chest. "Don't you miss the excitement and glamour of the corporate world?"

Kali felt a tendril of hair fall from the clip holding her hair off her neck. "Some days, but mostly when the goats are acting ornery."

"But how could you throw away a six-figure salary for goats?"

"In a word? Passion." Kali looked across the room and measured her professional satisfaction not in business suits or humming fax machines, but in creativity. "I discovered something about myself when Aunt Annalise became so ill. Life would be meaningless if on my deathbed all I had to look back on were legal documents and a bank account."

Lacy sighed. "I once heard a professor say follow your heart, not your checkbook."

Kali grinned. "I bet his speech made a real impression on college seniors. If someone had told me that ten years ago, I would have said, 'Oh, get real.'"

"That's my consensus too." Lacy picked a packaging logo from the pile on the table. "So what made you do it?"

"When I took Aunt Annalise back to her family in France, I saw firsthand how hand-pressed cheese was made and how superior it was to anything I'd ever eaten in those fancy D.C. restaurants. And . . . I fell in love." Kali wiped her hands on her apron. "I loved the smell of the farm in the mornings. I loved sensing the different flavors inherent in the goat milk. I connected to the rhythm of the process. And nothing proved more satisfying than serving someone a slice of cheese and seeing their eyes close in delirious pleasure."

"Your clients never showed delirious pleasure over a favorable verdict?"

"No, they usually grimaced and groaned as they wrote a check for my fees."

Lacy chuckled. "You were expensive."

"But I didn't get to see the money. It went into the corporate pot and was split among the firm. There was no conclusion for me. Of course I didn't know when I started that I'm the kind of person who needs the satisfaction of a completed cycle. And apparently I had issues with wanting to be my own boss."

"If only the goats would recognize you as their leader that would make things even better."

"I didn't count on them being quite so stubborn. Who knew Queenie would earn her name?" Kali moved the cheese molds to a cooling rack. "But at least when I lay my head down at night, I find myself at peace because I've made something. I've fulfilled a process. And the cheese gives pleasure to others. So that makes me happy too."

Lacy helped secure the rack from rolling onto the uneven floor. "I don't know that I can be happy making cheese for the rest of my life."

Kali wiped her hands on her apron before wrapping her arm around her sister's shoulders. "That's okay. Just because I'm happy with curds and whey doesn't mean you're supposed to feel the same. We're different. Even though we both grew up with Aunt Annalise singing 'Frère Jacques' doesn't mean we both like French songs. You're unique. You have your own special blend of pleasures and goals."

"But I majored in business, and I don't know what I'm supposed to do with my life."

"Cut yourself some slack, Lacy. You're only twenty-two—some people don't find out their true passions until they're forty or eighty. God knits these things into our souls, but that doesn't mean they're easily discovered."

"But you found what you wanted and you're only thirty."

Kali stepped away from Lacy, pushing her hands deep into her pockets. "It took a tragic death to help me see the difference between what made me joyful and what filled my days with occasional spurts of happiness. I spent a lot of time praying after I left France. I needed to know I wasn't walking away from a sure income because of a misguided dream. So I did both for a while. But practicing law by day and making cheese at night confirmed what I'd already suspected about myself. I yearned to own a farm. Buying Queenie became a purposeful act and not a whim."

"So how am I going to discover my passion?" Lacy winked. "Although I haven't ruled out the glamour of corporate America as easily as you did."

"You goof," Kali chided. "Maybe corporate life is your passion.

Maybe you're the kind of person that thrives on the process of putting together deals. Whatever you do, don't force the discovery of the gifts deep inside you. Let them emerge with time. Sometimes it's in the routine of life that we understand what gives us soul-satisfying pleasure."[6]

> *We cannot do everything at once,*
> *but we can do something at once.*
> **CALVIN COOLIDGE**
> *thirtieth U.S. president*

THE POWER OF POTENTIAL

What are your obligations and responsibilities? While being faithful to fulfill them, determine to use your "free" time to invest in the study of your dream. Even today, do a search on the Internet and see what nuggets you can find.

Little by little does the trick.
AESOP
ancient Greek author

Ninety-nine times the conclusion is false. The hundredth time I am right.
ALBERT EINSTEIN
twentieth-century American/German physicist

The little things are infinitely the most important.
ARTHUR CONAN DOYLE
twentieth-century British physician and novelist

WISDOM SPEAKS

I know my goals and I'm not giving up, but progress is so slow! Once I was out of school I thought I could move into the career I want. Why does it take so long? Each step is so tiny.

Little strokes fell great oaks.
BENJAMIN FRANKLIN
eighteenth-century American statesman and philosopher

Each of us has a fire in our hearts for something. It's our goal in life to find it and to keep it lit.
MARY LOU RETTON
American gymnast and Olympic gold medalist

Most people would succeed in small things if they were not troubled with great ambitions.
HENRY WADSWORTH LONGFELLOW
nineteenth-century American poet

Hope is a waking dream.
ARISTOTLE
fourth-century B.C. Greek philosopher

Large streams from little fountains flow, tall oaks from little acorns grow.
DAVID EVERETT
nineteenth-century American poet

The greatest masterpieces were once only pigments on a palette.
HENRY S. HASKINS
twentieth-century American writer

From a little spark may burst a mighty flame.
DANTE ALIGHIERI
fourteenth-century Italian author and poet

No one keeps up his enthusiasm automatically. Enthusiasm must be nourished with new actions, new aspirations, new efforts, new vision. Compete with yourself; set your teeth and dive into the job of breaking your own record. It is one's own fault if his enthusiasm is gone; he has failed to feed it.

AUTHOR UNKNOWN

*God will help you overflow
with hope
in him through the
Holy Spirit's power within you.*
ROMANS 15:13 TLB

You Mud, You Tape, and You Keep Going

Nancy Hoag

I pushed for years with no real success. "I'm writing a novel," I claimed in more than one Christmas letter. But the truth? I'd given it my best days *and* nights, even though I might have earned more at McDonald's. Now it was time to give up. But then suddenly my husband was announcing he'd also be retiring? "My wife has supported all of my career decisions," he wrote in his final dispatch. "It's her turn, she's an incredible writer." He'd be doing the laundry. "Cooking, too. Nothing gourmet, just meat and potatoes." But I wasn't to lift a finger. "Except to type," he laughed, hugging me.

Still, with this gift of time, I kept seeing dining-room dust and the cat smudges on the French doors. "At least let me vacuum—"

"Excuses," Scotty said, "you're stalling."

I wasn't; I was afraid. I'd created over five hundred manuscript pages and still hadn't reached "the end"—I'd become overwhelmed, even filing felt beyond me.

Until the afternoon I decided to visit our basement. Although my spouse retired from a desk job, he'd grown up on a ranch, and he knew how to use tools. He'd decided to frame in the duct work with eight-foot 2 x 2s cut into two-foot pieces. "Tedious," he admitted one evening. "I don't *want* to go down there," I'd see on his face each morning. But within weeks, the framing was finished. "So now I'll deal with the wiring, insulation, and drywall," he said, literally crawling into bed.

If you've never worked with drywall, you don't know it's *heavy*. Only once did a friend assist him, and that was the day Scotty discovered he couldn't get 4 x 8 sheets down our narrow stairwell. He'd be pulling up carpet, removing wooden risers, dropping drywall through the gaping hole he'd be creating.

Next, he rented a mechanical lift and wrestled it into his dwindling work space, surrounded by a Nordic Trak, inflatable boat, stacked books, and boxed dishes. He never said, "I love doing this." Never even hinted, "Like." He simply made a commitment to work from breakfast until bedtime. Then, with pain in his hands, arms, and shoulders, he'd lie on the floor while I ran the massager—week after week, with his fingers losing all sense of feeling, one hand swelling to nearly double its normal size.

Finally, after weeks of lifting and securing, he completed the drywall. Now he'd be applying layers of mud and tape and skimming and smoothing after every layer—even though I suggested, "It's good enough, no one's going to see it."

And I'd hear, "I've come this far . . . ," which meant he'd keep going, prepare the walls with primer, applying second and third coats.

And then the neighbors began to make an appearance. "How conscientious he is," one woman said. Another wondered would we consider selling. Suddenly, we were entertaining multiple offers. My husband's perseverance—though he hadn't always felt like persevering—was going to be rewarded.

And so will mine be . . . and yours.

Writing isn't easy, and going to school was even more difficult. But what about finishing an entire basement? "It won't get done by itself," Scotty said one morning. He hadn't been certain he could pull this off, he made mistakes, had torn some work out, started over, and drove to home-improvement centers with lengthy lists of problems.

Meanwhile, I continue to wrestle with my writing. I envision novels, but I also envision failing. There are still the loosely knit fragments, characters that haven't quite jelled. On the other hand, there are now over 1500 pages, there's a beginning and a middle, I've caught a brief glimpse of the end that will come after I've sufficiently touched up and refined . . . just as my husband prepared his project with framing, drywall, and finish for one long year. Like Scotty, I've made lists, and sought help from any expert I could corner. I've also made discoveries by trial and error.

Then one morning, I again entertained the thought of quitting. I filled two mugs with coffee and descended the stairs. "You don't have to keep going over that door," I said. How many times did he have to do this? "The lights will be low, we'll hang pictures—"

Scotty smiled.

Over the top of my cup, I smiled too. "Back upstairs?" I said.

"Back upstairs." My husband grinned.

"You're going to do this until it's right."

"Yup." Scotty chuckled. "And so will you."

"And so will I," I said, nodding back over my shoulder and taking two stairs at a time to head back to my study, knowing—whether we're mudding, typing, or pursuing our dreams—our jobs don't get done by themselves. But once we've given it *our* best, the joy and sense of satisfaction will come.[7]

Trust in the LORD, and do good;
Dwell in the land,
and feed on His faithfulness.
Delight yourself also in the LORD,
And He shall give you the desires of your heart.
Commit your way to the LORD,
Trust also in Him,
And He shall bring it to pass.

PSALM 37:3–5 NKJV

The best way to make your dreams come true is to wake up.
J. M. POWER

Dreams grow holy when put in action.
ADELAIDE PROCTOR
nineteenth-century English poet and activist

Reach high, for stars lie hidden in your soul.
Dream deep, for every dream precedes the goal.
PAMELA VAULL STARR
twentieth-century poet and writer

S O   W H A T   N O W ?

M A K E   A   P L A N

It could be that you now have a degree, but you aren't sure how to use it. Three words will get you there: research, research, research! Listed on the following page are fields of employment open to anyone with a general degree. See if any of them strike your passion and then research to find your next course of action. Do you have all the skills required? Will you need postgraduate work? What occupation do you sense a passion for? Make some notes.

PERSUASIVE/ENTERPRISING JOBS

For these occupations, you will need an outgoing, competitive personality with excellent communication skills. This is a competitive field to enter. Consider:

☐ Marketing   ☐ Estate Planning

☐ Advertising   ☐ Sales

☐ Public Relations   ☐ Purchasing Agent

☐ Tourism   ☐ Self-Employment!

PEOPLE-MANAGEMENT JOBS

For these occupations, you will need strong leadership skills, spoken communication skills, and stamina. You will need to be prepared to be mobile and work irregular hours. These aren't desk jobs and require doers rather than thinkers. They often offer early responsibility.

☐ Retail Management

☐ Hotel and Catering Management

☐ Production Management

☐ Prison Management

☐ Customs and Immigration

☐ Personnel Management

PROFESSIONAL JOBS

For these occupations, you will need good administrative, analytical, and math skills. Often further study is needed to pass demanding professional examinations. These are well-paid jobs, offering fast promotion.

- ☐ Banking
- ☐ Insurance
- ☐ Law
- ☐ Accounting
- ☐ Management
- ☐ Medicine
- ☐ Librarian
- ☐ Multimedia/Web Designer
- ☐ Secretary
- ☐ Information Scientist
- ☐ Market Researcher
- ☐ Technical Writer

NONPROFIT-SECTOR JOBS

These jobs require good administrative and writing skills. They are often found in the not-for-profit sector of the business world. They offer the best opportunities for service to the community.

- ☐ Civil Service
- ☐ Local Government
- ☐ Charity Fund-raising
- ☐ Armed Forces
- ☐ Animal Control
- ☐ Community Services
- ☐ Politics
- ☐ Firefighter
- ☐ Police Officer

SERVICE JOBS

These jobs require good social skills and usually a further full-time course of study.

- ☐ Teaching
- ☐ Social Work
- ☐ Probation Work
- ☐ Youth and Community Work
- ☐ Housing Management
- ☐ Career Consultant
- ☐ Nursing
- ☐ Occupational Therapy
- ☐ Hospice Work
- ☐ Veterinary Services

MEDIA JOBS

These jobs are very competitive to enter and maintain. You need to be pushy, determined to get in, and develop good people skills. Most of these jobs are not advertised. They will require diligent research and contact development.

- ☐ Journalism
- ☐ Radio and Television
- ☐ Acting
- ☐ Publishing
- ☐ Arts Administration
- ☐ Filmmaking

Of course, these categories are incomplete, but they should help you identify your passion and gift. If you still aren't certain, study them often. Pray over them. Ask God to strike a fire of passion in your heart.

A Change of Plans

Coleen P. Kenny

"I'm going to be a pediatric nurse," I told my mom.

"I'm going to be a pediatric nurse," I told the guidance counselor.

"I'm going to be a pediatric nurse," I told the nursing professor.

I'd set my sights on nursing after receiving a Hasbro Dolly's Nurse Kit complete with plastic stethoscope and cardboard eye chart when I was six. I'm not sure when I chose the pediatric track—maybe while babysitting the munchkin next door.

Fifteen years later, the first clinical rotation in nursing school landed ten of us on a pediatric unit. *The perfect place to start!* I thought.

We arrived at seven a.m. with real stethoscopes slung around the collars of our crisp white dresses (no caps, thank goodness), and we received our assignment for the day. After two years of liberal arts and textbook nursing classes, we were eager to get our hands on real live patients.

My imagination could not have conjured a day more different.

Nothing clicked. No bond formed with my tiny patient. No bond formed with the instructor who grew impatient with my lack of IV skills. Heck, I'd never set one up before. I was as miserable as a cat falling in a commode. I could not wait for those seven weeks to end. *What happened?* I thought. *Did I choose the wrong profession?*

The experience shoved my preconceived notions of pediatric nursing out the door and left me gun-shy of our next rotation: geriatrics. *I've never been to a nursing home. I have no grandparents. I don't know any old people. If the kids I dreamed about didn't fulfill my plan, how could this turn out any better?*

I arrived on the geriatric rehab unit with little enthusiasm. Finishing the semester and rethinking my major were my only goals.

A different instructor met us that sunny October morning. The third-floor nursing-station window framed a giant fireball of a maple tree, and the staff greeted us warmly. The unit didn't smell, and no one was moaning or tied down like in all the old movies.

We dispersed to our assigned rooms, and an elderly gentleman awaited this uncertain student. Mr. T, due to a stroke, needed help bathing and getting dressed, and he allowed me to practice making a bed with a full-size immobile man rather than the lightweight plastic mannequin from our practice lab. With the instructor's supervision I administered Mr. T's medications and took his blood pressure. The day moved as swiftly and smoothly as a ski on new snow, and I returned to my dorm without tears.

Excitement rather than dread accompanied me the following Tuesday. The instructor assigned ninety-year-old Mr. T to me again, so I listened to his report, then walked to his room, hoping to find out how his therapy was going.

Nothing could have prepared me for what I found. A slew of medical students and interns in long white coats surrounded Mr. T, fighting him to insert an IV and breathing tube. *What happened? What are they doing to my patient? What changed in the thirty minutes since the night nurse handed off her charge?*

Mr. T's struggle broke my heart. Reality-shocked, I froze in the doorway.

As Mr. T jerked his head to evade the breathing tube, his eyes locked on mine. Fingers clenching a cold metal bedrail stretched toward me. I stepped forward, and he grasped my hand with amazing strength. Staring into my eyes, his body relaxed, and the clinicians were able to complete their stabilizing work. I sat with Mr. T until the ambulance transported him to the acute-care facility.

The instructor assigned me another patient, but Mr. T remained in my mind. As the seven weeks progressed, I not only stopped rethinking my major, I applied and worked as a nurse's aide on the unit for the final two years of school, and I was present when Mr. T passed away. When I received my bachelor's degree and passed the RN licensure exam, the unit became home for the first two years of my career.

Since, I've been a head nurse in a nursing home, worked in home care, and after earning my master's degree and nurse practitioner certification, I have worked in long-term care for nine years and counting.

The elderly don't scare me anymore, and the gifts I receive on a daily basis from a profession I'd never even considered confirm my calling. Someone Else knew where I belonged and arranged the circumstances to get me here. So when new opportunities arise, I release my brain's preconceived notions and pray, *Show me.* And when people say, "How can you work with old people?" my reply is always the same: *How can I not?*[8]

W I S D O M   S P E A K S

I want to make a million dollars before the age of thirty. Do you have any advice to help me along the way?

I believe the power to make money is a gift from God . . . to be developed and used to the best of our ability for the good of mankind.

JOHN D. ROCKEFELLER
twentieth-century American businessman and self-made millionaire

To learn the value of money, it is not necessary to know the nice things it can get for you; you have to have experienced the trouble of getting it.

PHILIPPE HÉRIAT
twentieth-century French author

Money can buy the husk of many things, but not the kernel. It brings you food, but not appetite; medicine, but not health; acquaintances, but not friends; servants, but not faithfulness; days of joy, but not peace and happiness.

HENRIK IBSEN
nineteenth-century Norwegian playwright

Money has never yet made anyone rich.

SENECA
first-century Roman statesman, dramatist, and philosopher

[Jesus said]: Don't store up treasures here on earth, where moths eat them and rust destroys them, and where thieves break in and steal. Store your treasures in heaven, where moths and rust cannot destroy . . . Wherever your treasure is, there the desires of your heart will also be.

MATTHEW 6:19–21 NLT

I so want my family and friends to be proud of me. Sometimes I feel as if I should change my direction so I will not disappoint them. Is this wrong?

Almost every man wastes part of his life in attempts to display qualities, which he does not possess, and to gain applause, which he cannot keep.

SAMUEL JOHNSON
greatest English writer of the eighteenth century

Do not base your life on the judgments of others; first, because they are as likely to be mistaken as you are, and further, because you cannot know that they are telling you their true thoughts.

JEAN-JACQUES ROUSSEAU
eighteenth-century French philosopher

A wise unselfishness is not a surrender of yourself to the wishes of anyone, but only to the best discoverable course of action.

DAVID SEABURY
twentieth-century American author

If I trim myself to suit others, I will soon whittle myself away.

AUTHOR UNKNOWN

Be yourself—truthfully
Accept yourself—gracefully
Value yourself—joyfully
Forgive yourself—completely
Treat yourself—generously
Balance yourself—harmoniously
Bless yourself—abundantly
Trust yourself—confidently
Love yourself—wholeheartedly
Empower yourself—prayerfully
Give of yourself—enthusiastically
Express yourself—radiantly

AUTHOR UNKNOWN

Ballerina Dreams and Beautiful Realities

Alison Simpson

When I was a little girl, I wanted to be a ballerina. I took ballet classes and practiced all the time. I listened to classical music and made up ballet routines. I owned a book by Margo Fontayne and tried to emulate all her poses in my room. I *really* wanted to dance.

My parents knew this about me, and they willingly paid for ballet classes and all kinds of ballerina gear. My father was all about helping me discover my talent and my passion. In fact, as far back as I can remember, my father was always looking for that "thing" that created a spark in me. And he was always encouraging me to "do the thing you love."

But when I got a little older, reality won out when it came to my ballerina dream. The reality was, I just wasn't that graceful. And I certainly didn't have the lithe, fluid motions that it seemed I needed to have if I wanted to go further. And to be totally and completely honest, I just didn't really want to work at it anymore. So I stopped taking classes, put my Margo book on the shelf, and hung up my ballet shoes.

At about nine years old I started keeping a journal. It wasn't anything deep, just something that helped me work through challenges, thoughts about my life, and even just bad days. Soon, my writing included also poetry and short stories. And when I'd show my parents what I'd done, I could see it in their eyes . . . they thought it was good. Certainly not the work of a child prodigy, but it was good.

But even for all the writing I did, my parents were usually the only ones to see it. I didn't make a big deal out of it. In school I always got high marks for my writing. But I never wrote for accolades—I did it for me. Being a writer wasn't something that seemed realistic for my life. I guess I figured it was another ballerina dream. And by that time, I was really into music, and I figured that would be my career. In fact, I was convinced of it. This was my "thing" that my dad always talked about. I'd go to college and study music education, then get my certification in music therapy, and that would be my profession. It just made sense and I liked it. I even won a music scholarship to college and thought I was definitely on my way.

But no, that wasn't it either. I realized that during my sophomore year of college. I was sure that was not the direction for me. I declined my scholarship that year and changed my major to "undecided." I prayed, I studied all the different ways that God guides us, and I started searching myself—my dreams, my desires, what was realistic for me, and what was not. I found the answers in something that had long been like a best friend but not one I ever considered a realistic career—writing. I wrote a lot, that's for sure . . . but I never considered myself a writer.

So I declared myself a journalism major, and three years later I had earned my degree. And to this day I'm still writing, and I'm getting paid to do it. And it's still something I'd do even if I never got a penny for it.

Dreams and aspirations are beautiful and valuable. They awaken our minds and encourage us to look beyond our present circumstances to what we *could* be. And while we may never achieve all that we *could* be, we are motivated to work harder when we value our dreams. I love my dreams because they help me understand myself and appreciate myself. I know I won't achieve them all. But I *have* achieved some of them, and I'm very proud of myself for that. I didn't do it through any kind of intrinsic talent alone. I did it because I worked hard and I wanted it bad enough.

Sometimes "ballerina dreams" and "reality" are two different things. But sometimes they meld together with a unique combined reaction that will astound you in ways you never imagined. Don't be afraid to dream, but don't be afraid of reality. If you're looking to God for direction and allowing yourself to dream and also to be lucid about your life, you'll be living a beautiful reality . . . which is much better than just a "ballerina dream."[9]

Use your gifts faithfully,
and they shall be enlarged;
practice what you know, and you shall
attain to higher knowledge.

MATTHEW ARNOLD
nineteenth-century English poet and critic

THE POWER OF POTENTIAL

Identify an obstacle that stands between you and your life's dream. Is it time to detour or overcome? Ask God.

All our talents increase in the using, and every faculty, both good and bad, strengthens by exercise.

ANNE BRONTË
nineteenth-century English author

Those talents which God has bestowed upon us are not our own goods but the free gifts of God; and any persons who become proud of them show their ungratefulness.

JOHN CALVIN
sixteenth-century French theologian and reformer

Talent is God-given; be humble.
Fame is man-given; be grateful.
Conceit is self-given; be careful.

JOHN WOODEN
one of the greatest coaches in college basketball history

SAY YES TO WHAT MATTERS MOST

Becoming a Person
of Character

We make a living by what we get,
but we make a life by what we give.

SIR WINSTON CHURCHILL
twentieth-century British statesman

When first things are put first,
second things are not suppressed
but increased.

C. S. LEWIS
twentieth-century English novelist and essayist

Changing the World

I am only one, but still I am one. I cannot do everything, but still I can do something; and because I cannot do everything, I will not refuse to do something I can do.

EDWARD EVERETT HALE
orator and statesman, nephew of Nathan Hale

Every action in our lives touches on some chord that will vibrate in eternity.

EDWIN HUBBEL CHAPIN
nineteenth-century author, lecturer, and social reformer

Giving

We may give without loving, but we cannot love without giving. Work is love made visible.

AUTHOR UNKNOWN

You are never more like God, than when you give.

AUTHOR UNKNOWN

It's not how much you've given, but how much you've kept, that really matters.

AUTHOR UNKNOWN

If there be any truer measure of a man than by what he does, it must be by what he gives.

ROBERT SOUTH
eighteenth-century English clergyman

You're the only one who can make the difference. Whatever your dream is, go for it.

EARVIN "MAGIC" JOHNSON
considered one of the 50 greatest basketball players in NBA history

Share with God's people who are in need. Practice hospitality.

ROMANS 12:13

THE POWER OF POTENTIAL

List three things you can do to change your world. Make a plan to get started.

Do what good you can, and do it solely for God's glory, as free from it yourself as though you did not exist. Ask nothing whatever in return. Done in this way, your works are spiritual and godly.

MEISTER ECKHART
fourteenth-century German clergyman

A Christian should always remember that the value of his good works is not based on their number and excellence, but on the love of God which prompts him to do these things.

JOHN OF THE CROSS
sixteenth-century Catholic saint

If I Can Stop One Heart from Breaking

Emily Dickinson
beloved nineteenth-century American poet

If I can stop one heart from breaking,
I shall not live in vain;
If I can ease one life the aching,
Or cool one pain,
Or help one fainting robin
Into his nest again,
I shall not live in vain.

Since you have been chosen by God who has given you this new kind of life, and because of his deep love and concern for you, you should practice tenderhearted mercy and kindness to others. Don't worry about making a good impression on them but be ready to suffer quietly and patiently. Be gentle and ready to forgive; never hold grudges. Remember, the Lord forgave you, so you must forgive others.

Most of all, let love guide your life, for then the whole church will stay together in perfect harmony. Let the peace of heart which comes from Christ be always present in your hearts and lives, for this is your responsibility and privilege as members of his body. And always be thankful.

Remember what Christ taught and let his words enrich your lives and make you wise; teach them to each other and sing them out in psalms and hymns and spiritual songs, singing to the Lord with thankful hearts. And whatever you do or say, let it be as a representative of the Lord Jesus, and come with him into the presence of God the Father to give him your thanks.

Colossians 3:12–17 TLB

Words About Ideals

William Jennings Bryan
twentieth-century American lawyer and politician

An ideal is above price. It means the difference between success and failure—the difference between a noble life and a disgraceful career. If a man measures life by what others do for him, he is apt to be disappointed, but if he measures life by what he does for others, there is no time for despair. If he measures life by its accumulations, these usually fall short of his expectations, but if he measures life by the contribution which he has made to the sum of human happiness, his only disappointment is in not finding time to do all that his heart prompts him to do. Whether he spends his time trying to absorb from the world only to have the burden of life grow daily heavier, or spends his time in an effort to accomplish something of real value to the race, depends upon his ideal.

*Ideals are like tuning forks:
sound them often to bring
your life up to standard pitch.*
S. D. GORDON
early-twentieth-century author and speaker

Meet the Dream Weavers

If the British went out by water,
we would show two lanterns in the
North Church steeple; and if by land,
one . . .

Paul Revere

He languished in obscurity in the annals of American history before Henry Wadsworth Longfellow published a poem about him in 1861—almost one hundred years after his feat of bravery and cunning.

Born in 1734, Paul Revere grew up in Boston and learned the art of gold and silversmithing from his father. After his father died when Paul was nineteen, he took over the family business. While gaining recognition for his fine silversmithing work, Revere befriended several patriots involved in the cause against the British throne. Soon the fight for freedom outweighed his desire for security and success.

Revere's engravings of the 1770 Boston Massacre served as evidence in a subsequent trial prosecuting the British soldiers. He was likely present at the Boston Tea Party in 1773 as well. In the wake of that event, Britain closed the port of Boston and began amassing soldiers to quell the rebellion. About that time, Revere began making periodic rides to New York City and Philadelphia to deliver updates on the political unrest in Boston.

On the night of April 18, 1775, Paul Revere and his friend William Dawes embarked on their famous "Midnight Ride" from Boston to Lexington. They sought to warn John Hancock and Samuel Adams that the British army was marching toward

Lexington and was likely to arrest the two men and seize the weapon supplies in Concord. Duly warned, the patriots successfully defended themselves against the advancing troops.

After the Revolutionary War, Revere became renowned as a master metalworker. He spent the rest of his life involving himself in industry, politics, and community service. He died in 1818.

By sacrificing his security and success for what mattered most, in the long run, Paul Revere received the security and success he had originally enjoyed. And more.

> *Trust in the LORD, and do good;*
> *so you will live in the land and enjoy security.*
> PSALM 37:3 NRSV

Each time a person stands up for an ideal, or acts to improve the lot of others, or strikes out against injustice, he sends forth a tiny ripple of hope, and crossing each other from a million different centers of energy and daring, those ripples build a current which can sweep down the mightiest walls of oppression and injustice.

ROBERT FRANCIS KENNEDY
U.S. attorney general and brother of John F. Kennedy

Finally, brethren, whatever things are true, whatever things are noble, whatever things are just, whatever things are pure, whatever things are lovely, whatever things are of good report, if there is any virtue and if there is anything praiseworthy—meditate on these things.
PHILIPPIANS 4:8 NKJV

THE POWER OF POTENTIAL

Have you ever made a sacrifice for something you believe in? Taking a stand is not something you should do frivolously or in the absence of much prayer and thoughtfulness. But the time will come when you will feel the fire rise up in your soul and you'll know—this is my call to arms. When that day comes, give yourself completely, fearlessly, and go with God's grace and power to stand for what is right and good and just. It will likely be your greatest moment.

Be strong and courageous. Do not be terrified; do not be discouraged, for the LORD your God will be with you wherever you go.

JOSHUA 1:9

HOW TO HAVE WINNING RELATIONSHIPS

★ Reach out. Wait for others to reach out to you, and you might be waiting for a long time. Sure there is risk involved, but you can handle it.

★ Stay positive. No one wants to spend time with someone who is always whining and complaining. Focus on what's good in your life and the lives of others.

★ Don't hold grudges. No one is perfect, including you. So choose to overlook flaws and forgive easily—but be wise about toxic people.

★ Get over yourself. No one wants to hear you talk about yourself all the time. Put the focus on others, and you will never be lonely.

★ Be a good listener. It's the only way to really get to know someone, deep down where the important relationships are established and nourished.

★ Say you're sorry. You did it; you know you did it; make nice.

★ Value honesty. People can smell phoniness a mile away, so be yourself. Tell others the truth; just be sure you do it only when needed and with kindness and sensitivity.

★ Be there. The most important thing you can do for your friends is to share their happiness, applaud their achievements and good fortune, and be there to hold their hands when trouble comes.

Work

All work, even cotton-spinning, is noble; work is alone noble.
THOMAS CARLYLE
nineteenth-century Scottish essayist and historian

Work! God wills it. That, it seems to me, is clear.
GUSTAVE FLAUBERT
nineteenth-century French novelist

Eight hours for work, Eight hours for sleep,
Eight hours for what we will.
1866 SLOGAN FOR THE NATIONAL LABOR UNION OF THE UNITED STATES

All growth depends upon activity. There is no development physically or intellectually without effort, and effort means work. Work is not a curse; it is the prerogative of intelligence, the only means to adulthood, and the measure of civilization.
CALVIN COOLIDGE
thirtieth U.S. president

The average person puts only 25 percent of his energy and ability into his work. The world takes off its hat to those who put in more than 50 percent of their capacity, and stands on its head for those few and far between souls who devote 100 percent.
ANDREW CARNEGIE
nineteenth-century American industrialist and philanthropist

Too many of us become enraged because we have to bear the shortcomings of others. We should remember that not one of us is perfect, and that others see our defects as obviously as we see theirs. We forget too often to look at ourselves through the eyes of our friends. Let us, therefore, bear the shortcomings of each other for the ultimate benefit of everyone.

ABRAHAM LINCOLN
sixteenth U.S. president

THE POWER OF POTENTIAL

Have you ever stood up for something that you felt was right when no one else would? What happened?

What we have done for ourselves alone dies with us; what we have done for others and the world remains and is immortal.

ALBERT PIKE
nineteenth-century attorney, soldier, and writer

I pronounce it as certain that there was never a truly great man that was not at the same time truly virtuous.

BENJAMIN FRANKLIN
eighteenth-century American statesman and philosopher

Love Settles the Question

Sharon Gibson

"I don't *want* to live the American dream, Mom," my son announced to me one afternoon as we discussed his after-graduation plans. "I know I could stay in the U.S., get a good job, have a nice home and a car but that is not what is in my heart."

I looked at him in disbelief, fearing what was coming next.

Alex had worked hard to obtain his degree, and his achievements were miraculous considering what he'd had to overcome.

"I want to go back to the slums to help my brothers and sisters escape the abuse and poverty I left in Brazil," he continued.

Eight years ago, my husband and I adopted him from an orphanage in Brazil where he escaped the living hell of a slum there. His mother severely abused Alex, and he ran away from his home to an orphanage in a nearby neighborhood.

He settled in with us, finished high school, and attended a local university. He returned to Brazil on a summer business internship and located his biological family. He discovered he had seven brothers and sisters, five of them who were born after he left.

Now he wanted to return to Brazil again. I shifted my position as we sat on the living-room couch. I frowned, "Dad and I sacrificed for you to be able to have a better life. We did not have in mind for you to return to the slums of Brazil!" I drew a deep breath and sighed, "Brazil is a very long way from here, and I don't really want to be that far from you."

"Mom, I feel *God* has put this in my heart," he insisted. "My brothers and sisters *need* me. There are no opportunities for poor kids in Brazil."

I chewed on the end of my glasses as I considered his statements. Finally, I replied, "Who am I to stand in the way of God? If God has put that in your heart to do, then go for it."

His green eyes lit up as he looked at me and smiled. "Thanks, Mom, for understanding."

After graduation, he remained steadfast in his desire to return to Brazil. While his classmates got jobs in their chosen fields and pursued their careers, he set out to fulfill his dream.

That fall my husband and I accompanied Alex to Brazil to meet his brothers and sisters. While we were there, Alex visited with his sister and learned the abuse and neglect of the kids had escalated from two years ago.

Alex, filled with righteous anger, said, "That's it! I am going to the judge this week to file to have the children taken away from her."

Later that week, my husband, Alex, and I piled into a taxicab to head for the courthouse. I clung to the backseat as the driver hit as many potholes as he missed. I questioned whether we were doing the right thing. As if reading my thoughts, Alex said, "Mom, on the phone, the social worker said they had been looking for several months for someone to care for these kids."

As I looked at him, I heard the Lord say, *I am just looking for someone to take a stand for these kids.* A quote came to mind, "All it takes for evil to prevail is for good men to do nothing." I knew then we had to support our son in his unusual choice regardless of where this journey took us.

Alex obtained temporary custody and decided to stay in Brazil until he could get the permanent guardianship of Michelle, fourteen; Ingrid, nine; Michael, eight; and then bring them to the United States. Together, they moved into a small two-room house.

In the midst of the intensity of the court fight in Brazil with the mother and the challenge of caring for the children, I called him on the phone. He confided in me, "This is more difficult than I thought. I really miss you, Dad, the U.S., and my friends. I realize one thing—love is about sacrifice. When I wonder if I made the right choice, I look at the kids now compared to when I first got them and I see God's purpose for them and for me. It's worth it."

God calls each of us to change the world. We think an education is a *guarantee* of the "good life." Maybe we need to think of an education as *preparation* to change the world.

While for some it may not be as extreme as Alex's sacrifice, it is in our best interest to yield our plans, gifts, and talents to God. Only God knows the paths that will guide us to our destiny, meet the needs of others, and satisfy the desires of our heart.[10]

He who will live for others shall have great troubles, but they shall seem to him small. He who will live for himself shall have small troubles, but they shall seem to him great.

WILLIAM R. INGE
twentieth-century American playwright

Meet the Dream Weavers

*We can overcome evil with
greater good.*

Former first lady Laura Bush

"Behind every great man," the adage goes, "there is a great
woman." Some women hover over their men, prodding them to
pursue uninspired dreams that will never be fulfilled. Other women
embody a sense of grace that inspires others to greatness.

Laura Bush is one of those women.

Born on November 4, 1946, Laura Welch Bush grew up in
Midland, Texas. Inspired by her second-grade teacher, she attended
Southern Methodist University, earning a degree in education in
1968. She then taught in the Dallas and Houston public schools.
In 1973, she earned a master of library science degree from the
University of Texas. She then remained in Austin and worked as a
librarian in the public schools.

In 1977, Laura met George Bush at a backyard barbecue. At the
time, he owned an oil company, but it quickly became apparent
that he also held very high political aspirations. When George
proposed to the painfully shy Laura, she agreed to marry him on
one condition: that she would never be asked to make a speech
for a political campaign. Three months after their first date, they
married.

After the birth of her twin daughters, Barbara and Jenna, in
1981, Laura recognized that George's heavy drinking was negatively
affecting their family. Her influence convinced him to give up
alcohol in 1986. Throughout their marriage, Laura has had a steady
and calming influence on her husband.

In 1995, George Bush was elected governor of Texas. Despite her shyness and her husband's promise not to ask her to speak in public, George's increasing public presence forced her to become a more public person. Laura used her newfound confidence to promote various women's and children's causes, as well as literacy and libraries.

In 2000, Laura became the first lady of the United States. Since then, she has focused her efforts on education and women's health issues and launched the first National Book Festival.

Although the opinion polls regarding her husband have waxed and waned, Laura has consistently garnered high marks. Laura Bush was named the second most powerful woman in the United States (after Condoleezza Rice) and the fourth most powerful in the world by *Forbes* magazine in 2004.

A woman of grace who inspires others to greatness is an accurate description of Laura Bush.

When I called, you answered me;
you made me bold and stouthearted.
PSALM 138:3

THE POWER OF POTENTIAL

Are you destined for greatness? Most of us could never imagine what God has in store for us. If fame comes your way, if the path God has for you leads to a position of power and influence, remember that you are there according to God's calling. Determine first and most importantly to please Him in all you do.

The greatness of a man's power is the measure of his surrender.
WILLIAM BOOTH
founder of the Salvation Army

Be very careful, then, how you live—not as unwise but as wise, making the most of every opportunity.
EPHESIANS 5:15–16

Those prepared to do love's service will receive her rewards: new comfort and new strength.
HADEWIJCH
early thirteenth-century Dutch poet

FAMILY RELATIONSHIPS

IT'S ALL RELATIVE

No man will be respected by others who is despised by his own relatives.
PLAUTUS
ancient Roman dramatist and writer

Visit your aunt, but not every day; and call at your brother's, but not every night.
BENJAMIN FRANKLIN
eighteenth-century American statesman and philosopher

Unless [our love and care for our families] is a high priority, we may find that we may gain the whole world and lose our own children.
MICHAEL GREEN
author and Christian apologist

The happiest moments of my life have been the few which I have passed at home in the bosom of my family.
THOMAS JEFFERSON
third U.S. president

All the wealth in the world cannot be compared with the happiness of living together happily united.
MARGARET D'YOUVILLE
eighteenth-century Catholic saint

Jesus said to him, "I am the way, the truth, and the life. No one comes to the Father except through Me."
JOHN 14:6 NKJV

He who serves his brother best gets nearer God than all the rest.
ALEXANDER POPE
eighteenth-century English poet

What Does Love Look Like?

Saint Augustine
fifth-century Catholic saint

It has hands to help others.
It has feet to hasten to the poor and needy.
It has eyes to see misery and want.
It has ears to hear the sighs and sorrows of men.
That is what love looks like.

Blessed is the servant who loves his brother as much when he is sick and useless as when he is well and can be of service to him. And blessed is he who loves his brother as well when he is afar off as when he is by his side, and who would say nothing behind his back he might not, in love, say before his face.
SAINT FRANCIS OF ASSISI
thirteenth-century Italian friar

The Only Way to Have a Friend
Author Unknown

The only way to have a friend
Is to be one yourself;
The only way to keep a friend
Is to give from that wealth.

For friendship must be double fold,
Each one must give his share
Of feeling true if he would reap
The blessings that are there.

If you would say, "He is my friend,"
Then nothing else will do
But you must say, "I am his friend,"
And prove that fact be true.

We have mutual faults; neither of us is perfect; nothing in the form of humanity is perfect; let us, then, be kind to each other—forbearing, forgiving each other's faults—and above all, let us live in happiness and peace together.

HENRY CLAY, *nineteenth-century American statesman and orator from the Compromise Speech of 1850*

F R I E N D S H I P

B U I L D   R E L A T I O N S H I P S

So long as we love, we serve; so long as we are loved by others I would almost say that we are indispensable; and no man is useless while he has a friend.
ROBERT LOUIS STEVENSON
nineteenth-century Scottish novelist

If a man does not make new acquaintances as he advances through life, he will soon find himself alone. Man should keep his friendships in constant repair.
SAMUEL JOHNSON
eighteenth-century English lexicographer and author

By friendship you mean the greatest love; the greatest usefulness, the most open communication, the noblest sufferings, the severest truth, the heartiest counsel, and the greatest union of minds of which brave men and women are capable.
JEREMY TAYLOR
seventeenth-century English prelate and author

The glory of friendship is not the outstretched hand, nor the kindly smile nor the joy of companionship; it is the spiritual inspiration that comes to one when he discovers that someone else believes in him and is willing to trust him.
RALPH WALDO EMERSON
nineteenth-century American essayist and poet

CHOOSING YOUR FRIENDS

The people you spend your time with can make you or break you. Choose carefully.

★ **CHARACTER COUNTS.** Don't kid yourself. If you treat others with disdain, are careless with the truth, or can't be trusted to do the right thing, your relationships will eventually come back and bite *you!*

★ **CONSIDER VARYING INTERESTS AND LIFESTYLES.** If you happen to enjoy spending time at home in quiet pursuits, it would be unwise to choose a friend who loves to be on the move. Sure, you can share some good times together, but in the end, you'll disappoint each other.

★ **AVOID CONTROLLERS.** These are the people who want to be your *only* friend. They always have something to tell you about what your *other* friends think of you. These folks are toxic.

★ **LOOK FOR BALANCE.** In good relationships, friends take care of each other. Avoid relationships where you do all the caretaking.

★ **BE OPEN.** Don't make the mistake of thinking your friends must look like you, think like you, and speak like you. Great friends come in all shapes, sizes, ages, economic levels, and nationalities.

There is no truth more thoroughly established than that there exists in the economy and course of nature an indissoluble union between virtue and happiness, between duty and advantage. The propitious smiles of Heaven can never be expected on a nation that disregards the eternal rules of order and right, which Heaven itself has ordained.
GEORGE WASHINGTON
first U.S. president

Truth is always the strongest argument.
SOPHOCLES
fifth-century B.C. Greek dramatist

Let us not be blind to our differences—but let us also direct attention to our common interests and to the means by which those differences can be resolved. And if we cannot end now our differences, at least we can help make the world safe for diversity.
JOHN F. KENNEDY
thirty-fifth U.S. president

There never were, in the world, two opinions alike, no more than two hairs, or two grains; the most universal quality is diversity.
MICHEL DE MONTAIGNE
sixteenth-century French essayist

The Art of Giving

You get the best out of others when you give the best of yourself.

HARVEY S. FIRESTONE
American industrialist and founder of Firestone Tire and Rubber Co.

There is a wonderful mythical law of nature that the three things we crave most in life—happiness, freedom, and peace of mind—are always attained by giving them to someone else.

PEYTON CONWAY MARCH
twentieth-century general and former Army Chief of Staff

Some people give time, some money, some their skills and connections, some their life's blood, but everyone has something to give.

BARBARA BUSH
former first lady

The happiest people are those who give the most happiness to others.

DENIS DIDEROT
eighteenth-century French philosopher

Just Listen

Sue Rhodes Dodd

Fresh out of college, I landed my first job: a junior newspaper reporter with a Midwest daily. Lacking real-world experience, I was usually stuck reporting weather, calendar events, spelling bees, births, and deaths. Secretly I dreamed of getting cloak-and-dagger back-alley news tips, scooping the competing daily with my investigative reports, and winning acclaim from my peers for compelling stories redirecting the course of history. But my duties were more mundane, and I grew comfortable with the day-to-day routine.

One afternoon, the phone at the obituary desk rang, and I was the only one nearby. I answered it. "Newsroom."

"Uh, yeah, hello—I—gotta report a death."

Sitting down and reaching for pencil and paper, I started taking down the usual information listed in the obit column: name of deceased, age, address, etc. I had been through the routine so many times I could do it in my sleep.

"Cause of death?"

"Carbon monoxide poisoning."

"Self-inflicted?"

"Yeah."

"Time of death?"

After a long silence, the caller answered. "Well, I'm not sure yet."

My mind snapped out of its boredom into full alert. I started listening intently to the caller, my heart pounding. I asked the caller, "Do . . . you mean . . . the person hasn't . . . died yet?"

"Uh, yeah . . . but . . . dead . . . soon."

I waved over the assistant editor and scrawled a note: *Suicide caller.* The editor whispered, "I'll call the police. You keep 'em on the line."

Adrenaline pulsed through my veins, sharpening my focus and attention. Even though I was a lowly cub reporter, a life-and-death drama had just dropped into my lap.

"You said the deceased's name is Joe, right?"

By now, the caller's words were beginning to slur. "Uh—yeah—Joe."

Gently I asked, "That's your name, isn't it?"

With a snicker, he said yes. I was rocked by the realization that someone would willingly take his own life. Someone I was talking to, who was still very much alive at that moment. "Joe, tell me about the carbon monoxide. Where is that coming from?"

"I turned on . . . all the . . . uh . . . burners on the stove—no fire. I'm just feeling a little sleepy."

"Oh now, Joe, don't go to sleep," I said. Fighting back panic, I tried gently coercing him, "Joe, stay with me. I'd like to talk to you some more."

"Yeah . . . sure. That would be nice."

The city desk became a frenzy of activity as the assistant editor called police with the man's address. Sensing the drama, a group of reporters and editors gathered near my desk. I shut my eyes so I wouldn't be distracted by their stares. But there was no ignoring the banging of my own heart as I tried to keep Joe talking. Talking, talking about anything. How he lost his job. How his wife had left him.

"There's—just no reason—to—um–live." It was getting harder to understand what Joe was saying.

"Joe? Are you still there?"

"Yeah—hey—h—h—hold on."

Fighting panic, I pressed the phone against my ear. I strained to listen but couldn't decipher sounds on the other end of the phone. What could be happening? Inside I screamed, *Joe! Live! Please, God, don't let him die!* Without realizing it, I had stood up, the phone still to my ear.

Then, a different voice picked up the phone, and I asked, "Is Joe all right?"

"Sort of," the voice responded. "There's gas everywhere. I'm a police officer. We're all getting out of here. Thanks for calling us."

"Oh, no, thank *you*," I said, gently hanging up the phone as locked-up tears finally made their escape. The usually noisy newsroom had grown silent as a morgue.

I looked up at the crowd of reporters and murmured, "They got there in time."

The newsroom erupted into cheers, but I felt numb. A crisis abated, my coworkers seemed to breathe a collective sigh of relief and went back to their own stories and dramas and phone calls and deadlines. I sank back down in my chair, still stunned by the whole ordeal. Never had I imagined a seemingly insignificant job could touch the core of something that matters so much—life itself!

A single tear made its way down my cheek as I prayed, *Lord, help me never to squander a "chance" meeting. If You want me to do something—large or small—help me to pay attention and do it right.*[11]

THE POWER OF POTENTIAL

The important moments in life have a way of sneaking up on you. How can you prepare yourself for those critical moments that show your true character?

I hope I shall possess firmness and virtue enough to maintain what I consider the most enviable of all titles, the character of an honest man.

GEORGE WASHINGTON
first U.S. president

You will find as you look back on your life that the moments when you have really lived are the moments when you have done things in the spirit of love.

HENRY DRUMMOND
twentieth-century Canadian poet

I will not just live my life. I will not just spend my life. I will invest my life.

HELEN KELLER
twentieth-century American deafblind lecturer and author

If you wish to be fully alive you must develop a sense of perspective.

ANTHONY DE MELLO
twentieth-century Jesuit priest

A Day Worth While

Author Unknown

I count that day as wisely spent
In which I do some good
For someone who is far away
Or shares my neighborhood.
A day devoted to the deed
That lends a helping hand
And demonstrates a willingness
To care and understand.
I long to be of usefulness
In little ways and large
Without a selfish motive
And without the slightest charge.
Because in my philosophy
There never is a doubt
That all of us here on earth
Must help each other out.
I feel that day is fruitful
And the time is worth the while
When I promote the happiness
Of one enduring smile.

Meet the Dream Weavers

Surplus wealth is a sacred trust which its possessor is bound to administer in his lifetime for the good of the community.

Andrew Carnegie

Andrew Carnegie came with his family to America from Scotland in 1848. His father, Will, worked in a cotton factory as a weaver. Andrew drew his pay there, too, as a bobbin boy earning a whopping $1.20 per week! Who could imagine that this unassuming immigrant boy would one day become a multimillionaire who used his wealth to build thousands of libraries, schools, and colleges?

Andrew's family settled in Allegheny City, Pennsylvania, when he was thirteen years old. The trip from Scotland had been arduous, but an adventure. It was a journey that taught the boy how to face the unknown and work toward the future.

Hours in the cloth factory were long and conditions wretched. There was little time for Andrew to read, and, of course, books were scarce. There were never enough books to satisfy the young boy's heart and mind.

Soon he found a better job as a telegraph messenger boy and later became a telegraph operator. Next, he worked as a clerk for the Pennsylvania Railroad in Pittsburgh, working up to the position of train dispatcher. At twenty-four he began investing in stock. It was a humble beginning for a young man who would one day be considered one of the richest men in the world.

Carnegie made his fortune in the steel business. First, he became involved in iron factories and invested his money wisely. Then he learned about the Bessemer process of making steel from iron and set out to establish two steel factories in Pennsylvania. Carnegie was a visionary. He realized that the age of iron was passing. Steel, more flexible and lighter, was the material of the future. It would be needed to meet the needs of an expanding nation—for railroads, bridges, ships, and skyscrapers. The Carnegie Steel Company became a leader in the industry, and Carnegie became a vastly wealthy individual.

He was also a bighearted man. Many Americans have benefited from his generosity. Seven thousand churches received pipe organs that Carnegie paid for. Schools and colleges worldwide were funded from his pocket. Carnegie's passion was to provide the free use of books for hungry-minded young people to read. Children across the nation have happily browsed shelves full of books that Carnegie helped provide for them. Three thousand libraries were built for children whom he would never see or know. Carnegie believed his wealth should be used to help others. What a legacy!

> *Give freely and spontaneously. Don't have a stingy heart.*
> DEUTERONOMY 15:10 MSG

THE POWER OF POTENTIAL

Celebrate every success by making an investment in someone else's dream. Pitch in with whatever you have—money, time, hard-earned wisdom, creative ideas, encouragement.

It is possible to give freely and become more wealthy, but those who are stingy will lose everything.
PROVERBS 11:24 NLT

Meet the Dream Weavers

It was in the train I heard the call
to give up all and follow Him to
the slums to serve Him among the
poorest of the poor.

Mother Teresa

The homeless, disease ridden, poor, and wretched—these were the people Mother Teresa longed to help. Serving God as a Catholic nun, she took her faith to the streets to rescue the perishing and love the unlovable.

Born Agnes Gonxha Bojaxhiu in Yugoslavia in 1910, she left home at eighteen to join the Sisters of Loreto in Dublin. It was then she took the name Teresa, after Saint Teresa of Ávila and Thérèse of Lisieux, the patroness of missionaries. Later, she gained still another title, *"the saint of the gutters."*

As a novitiate of the order in Dublin, she learned English and then moved to Calcutta, India, where she taught history to young women for fifteen years.

In 1946 she went to Darjeeling to recover from tuberculosis. It was aboard the train that she heard God's call. After securing permission from Rome, she left the convent and headed for the slums.

She was willing to tend to the poorest and weakest—those sick and old who were abandoned in the streets of Calcutta to die. She searched for them and carried them in her arms to her home where she tended each like she would have tended her own parents. She nursed the diseased, comforted the dying, and fed and cared for outcasts—cripples and lepers.

In 1950 she started the Missionaries of Charity, a group of nuns who also had hearts to work with the sick and dying. Mother Teresa started her first home for the dying in Calcutta and later a leper colony. She established many orphanages, hospitals, and treatment centers. Mother Teresa became ill with heart disease and died in 1997, yet the order she led carries on the work among the poor.

Mother Teresa followed her passion to serve God by serving those who couldn't help themselves.

[Jesus said,] "I tell you the truth, whatever you did for one of the least of these brothers of mine, you did for me."
MATTHEW 25:40

THE POWER OF POTENTIAL

It's much easier to reach out to those we love than to lend a hand to an unlovely stranger. Volunteer for a day at a homeless shelter or soup kitchen. It is a kindness that God takes very personally.

Character is made by many acts; it may be lost by a single one.
AUTHOR UNKNOWN

A man is what he thinks about all day long.
RALPH WALDO EMERSON
nineteenth-century American essayist and poet

C H A R A C T E R

> **The qualities that distinguish you from all others.**

Out of our beliefs are born deed; out of our deed we form habits; out of our habits grow our character; and on our character we build our destiny.

HENRY HANCOCK
nineteenth-century English surgeon

Character may be manifested in the great moments, but it is made in the small ones.

PHILLIP BROOKS
nineteenth-century American bishop

Our character is but the stamp on our souls of the free choices of good and evil we have made through life.

JOHN CUNNINGHAM GEIKIE
twentieth-century Scottish clergyman

The quality of a person's life is in direct proportion to their commitment to excellence, regardless of their chosen field of endeavor.

VINCE LOMBARDI
one of the most successful coaches in National Football League history

Reputation is what men and women think of us. Character is what God and the angels know of us.

THOMAS PAINE
eighteenth-century American politician, philosopher, and author

The man who knows right from wrong and has good judgment and common sense is happier than the man who is immensely rich!

PROVERBS 3:13 TLB

INTEGRITY

Adhering to high moral standards.

Integrity without knowledge is weak and useless, and knowledge without integrity is dangerous and dreadful.

SAMUEL JOHNSON
greatest English writer of the eighteenth century

We arrive at the truth, not by the reason only, but also by the heart.

BLAISE PASCAL
seventeenth-century mathematician and philosopher

There is no such thing as a minor lapse of integrity.

TOM PETERS
career business coach

Never esteem anything as of advantage of thee that shall make thee break thy word or lose thy self-respect.

MARCUS AURELIUS ANTONINUS
Roman emperor

Show yourself in all respects a model of good works, and in your teaching show integrity.

TITUS 2:7 NRSV

Take care not knowingly to do or say anything which, if everyone were to know of it, you could not own, and say, "Yes, that is what I did or what I said."

LOUIS IX OF FRANCE
thirteenth-century king of France

Meet the Dream Weavers

I have never been lost,
but I will admit to
being confused for several weeks.

Daniel Boone

Although important, education does not guarantee success or significance. Some people attain the best education and do nothing with it. Others receive little or no education but make the most of it.

Daniel Boone was a hunter and explorer whose travels and exploits made him the most famous frontiersman in American history.

Born in 1734, Boone spent his early years on the western edge of the Pennsylvania frontier before moving to North Carolina. From the day his father gave him a gun at age twelve, Daniel Boone lived to hunt and explore—learning his skills from the local frontiersmen and Indians.

Because he spent so much time hunting during his youth, Boone received little formal education. Nevertheless, he overcame his educational barriers to become a knowledgeable, albeit unrefined, leader. He eventually taught himself to read and entertained other illiterate frontiersmen by reading to them around the campfire.

Daniel Boone hunted and explored the uncharted regions of North Carolina, Virginia, and Kentucky—what was considered the outpost of the American frontier. He also founded Boonesborough, the first white settlement in Kentucky.

In 1784 historian John Filson published a book depicting Boone as a cagy, adventurous folk hero. The book made the woodsman and explorer an overnight sensation across America and Europe. He eventually settled in Missouri and died in 1820 at the age of eighty-five. Daniel Boone served three terms in the Virginia state legislature, earning the respect of the American people—all without a formal education. He simply did what came naturally, what God had placed in his heart to do, what mattered most to him. That's all that is asked of anyone.

With God's power working in us, God can do much, much more than anything we can ask or imagine.

EPHESIANS 3:20 NCV

THE POWER OF POTENTIAL

Your gifts and talents are best used when they are committed to God. When you feel it is settled in your heart, write out a brief contract stating that you want to use your gifts as He would see fit, under the direction of the Holy Spirit. Then sign your name and date the document.

He who labors as he prays lifts his heart to God with his hands.

SAINT BERNARD OF CLAIRVAUX
twelfth-century Catholic saint

Virtue is not hereditary.

THOMAS JEFFERSON
third U.S. president

Clothe yourselves with compassion, kindness, humility, gentleness and patience. Bear with each other and forgive whatever grievances you may have against one another. . . . And over all these virtues put on love, which binds them all together in perfect unity.

COLOSSIANS 3:12–14

Let integrity and uprightness preserve me; for I wait on thee.

PSALM 25:21 KJV

Virtue is doing good to mankind in obedience to the will of God, and for the sake of everlasting happiness.

WILLIAM PALEY
eighteenth-century English theologian and philosopher

I must stand with anybody that stands right; stand with him while he is right, and part with him when he goes wrong.

ABRAHAM LINCOLN
sixteenth U.S. president

Meet the Dream Weavers

Injustice anywhere is a threat to justice everywhere.

Dr. Martin Luther King Jr.

Martin Luther King Jr., or M.L., as he was called, was a preacher's kid. He and his brother, Alfred Daniel, grew up in the house where they were born in Atlanta, Georgia. Martin was such a precocious child that his mother tried to get him into school when he was only five, but he was refused entry. Despite the setback, Martin advanced rapidly through school. He was ready for college when he was only fifteen.

Young Martin had an inner drive that made him push himself to get an education. He planned to be a preacher like his father and grandfather before him.

While M.L. was putting the finishing touches on his advanced degrees and educational goals, he returned to his father's pastorate in Atlanta, Ebenezer Baptist Church, where he was ordained and where he pastored alongside his father. This was what he had worked toward and dreamed about. But God's dreams for Martin were much broader than one congregation.

Martin Luther King Jr. became a pivotal figure in the fight for civil rights in America in the fifties and sixties. He led in the fight for reform and justice in America's southern states, which suffered from generations of prejudice. King also inspired change with his famed "I have a dream" speech, in which he expressed the dream of millions of Americans—the dream that one day we would all live in harmony with one another and future generations would judge others not by the color of their skin, but by their character.

A strong proponent of nonviolence, King encouraged his followers to wield words rather than guns. Linking arms with those who had a passion for change, he led them through one city and then another and straight into the pages of history. And when he spoke, wherever he spoke, his words pierced the conscience of the nation.

King believed in what he fought for and many times suffered humiliation and often even arrest for taking part in nonviolent demonstrations, which were meant to call attention to the wrong of discrimination and bring about change.

Dr. King was assassinated in 1968, in Memphis, Tennessee, where he had gone to help workers protest low pay and poor conditions. He had given his all to work toward equal rights for blacks in America. The Civil Rights Acts of 1957, 1960, and 1964, along with the 1965 Voting Rights Act, and the 1968 Fair Housing Act were the beginnings of integration and freedom for all Americans. A man with a passion for justice changed the face of the nation.

You need to persevere so that when you have done the will of God, you will receive what he has promised. For in just a very little while, "He who is coming will come and will not delay."
HEBREWS 10:36–37

THE POWER OF POTENTIAL

You have the potential to bring about change in your world. What cause could you get behind completely and wholeheartedly? What injustice fills you with passion? Ask God to show you how you can become part of the answer to the problem you see.

The lines of purpose in your lives never grow slack, tightly tied as they are to your future in heaven, kept taut by hope.

COLOSSIANS 1:5 MSG

WISDOM SPEAKS

I'm so happy to be finished with papers, tests, and grades, but how will I judge my success in the "real world"?

Success is to be measured not so much by the position that one has reached in life as by the obstacles which he has overcome.

BOOKER T. WASHINGTON
nineteenth-century American educator

Success is peace of mind, which is a direct result of knowing you did your best to become the best that you are capable of becoming.

JOHN WOODEN
one of the greatest coaches in college basketball history

Success based on anything but internal fulfillment is bound to be empty.

DR. MARTHA FRIEDMAN

A successful man is he who receives a great deal from his fellow men, usually incomparably more than corresponds to his service to them. The value of a man, however, should be seen in what he gives, and not in what he is able to receive.

ALBERT EINSTEIN
twentieth-century American/German physicist

H O W   T O   T A K E   A   S T A N D

Making a difference in your world

★ Talk through your feelings with God about the issue in question. Unless He is in your efforts, they will count for nothing.

★ Do your homework. Sometimes we think we understand an issue when in reality we don't. Research the issue from all sides to ensure that your views are well-balanced.

★ Ask for advice from the wise people around you. Remember, wise people come in all ages, shapes, and sizes.

★ Look into the pages of your Bible. You will almost certainly be surprised to discover insight, wisdom, and understanding in the pages of God's Word.

★ Get involved gradually, taking on one small responsibility at a time. If your passion rises, you'll know you've found your voice.

A good character carries with it the highest power of causing a thing to be believed.

ARISTOTLE
ancient Greek philosopher

A man never shows his own character so plainly as by the way he describes another's.

PAUL W. POWELL
American clergyman

Character is not in the mind. It is in the will.

FULTON JOHN SHEEN
twentieth-century American Catholic bishop

Resolved, to live with all my might while I do live. Resolved, never to lose one moment of time, to improve it in the most profitable way I can. Resolved, never to do anything which I should despise or think meanly in another. Resolved, never to do anything out of revenge. Resolved, never to do anything which I should be afraid to do if it were the last hour of my life.

LORD ARTHUR JAMES BALFOUR
twentieth-century British philosopher and statesman

Meet the Dream Weavers

*If I hadn't been sick I never would
have fought so hard just to keep
up. I developed a fight and drive
inside of me and the never-give-up
type of spirit that was needed for
a champion. God took something
meant for evil and turned it into
something good for my benefit
and His glory.*

Madeline Manning-Mims

Most people won't mind telling you they despise suffering. But
for some people, their suffering only makes them stronger.

Madeline Manning-Mims was born in Cleveland, Ohio, in
1948. When only three years of age, Madeline was diagnosed
with spinal meningitis and given little hope of surviving. Her
doctors warned her mother that if she lived, she would be mentally
impaired and unable to live a normal life.

But little Madeline's mother was a woman of prayer. She
dedicated her sickly daughter to God and promised to raise her
to follow Jesus. The physical challenge was indeed daunting, and
Madeline needed fourteen years to recover. But rather than impair
her, Madeline's sickness compelled her to excel beyond the other
children her age. While a sophomore in high school, Madeline took
a physical-fitness test and discovered that she was in top physical
condition, attaining one of the highest scores in the country.
Immediately, the coaches in her school recruited her for their teams.

Manning-Mims excelled particularly in track and field. While
in high school, she participated in the U.S. Nationals and became

the first woman in the world to run the 440-yard dash in fifty-five seconds flat.

In her senior year she was offered a full scholarship to Tennessee State. Between 1967 and 1981, Manning-Mims set women's world records in the 880-yard dash and won ten national track titles. She participated in the 1968, 1972, and 1976 Olympic Games, winning a gold and silver medal.

Since retiring from track, she has ministered to women in prisons across the country, and formed the Friends Fellowship, a ministry to female inmates. She's currently involved in sports chaplaincy, introducing world-class athletes to Christ and helping others grow in their faith.

Madeline Manning-Mims's bout with meningitis proves the apostle Paul's words that "[Christ's] power is made perfect in weakness" (2 Corinthians 12:9).

The LORD is my strength and my shield;
my heart trusts in him, and I am helped.
PSALM 28:7

From *Pilgrim's Progress*

John Bunyan
seventeenth-century English author

He that is down needs fear no fall;
He that is low, no pride;
He that is humble ever shall
Have God to be his guide.

THE POWER OF POTENTIAL

What matters most to God is—you! Does that surprise you? It's not your talent or your physical prowess or your intelligence or any other physical or mental attribute. He loves you and cares for you because you are His creation. Ask God how you can thank Him by using your gifts and talents for His glory.

Kings take pleasure in honest lips; they value a man who speaks the truth.
PROVERBS 16:13

A Character-Building Letter

*From: Paul, in jail for preaching the
Good News about Jesus Christ, and
from Brother Timothy.*

*To: Philemon, our much loved fellow
worker, and to the church that
meets in your home . . .*

May God our Father and the Lord Jesus Christ give you his blessings and his peace.

I always thank God when I am praying for you . . . because I keep hearing of your love and trust in the Lord Jesus and in his people. And I pray that as you share your faith with others it will grip their lives too, as they see the wealth of good things in you that come from Christ Jesus. I myself have gained much joy and comfort from your love, my brother, because your kindness has so often refreshed the hearts of God's people.

Now I want to ask a favor of you. I could demand it of you in the name of Christ because it is the right thing for you to do, but I love you and prefer just to ask you—I, Paul, an old man now, here in jail for the sake of Jesus Christ. My plea is that you show kindness to my child Onesimus, whom I won to the Lord while here in my chains. Onesimus (whose name means "Useful") hasn't been of much use to you in the past, but now he is going to be of real use to both of us. I am sending him back to you, and with him comes my own heart.

I really wanted to keep him here with me while I am in these chains for preaching the Good News, and you would have been helping me through him, but I didn't want to do it without your consent. I didn't want you to be kind because you had to but because you wanted to. Perhaps you could think of it this way: that he ran away from you for a little while so that now he can be yours forever, no longer only a slave, but something much better—a beloved brother, especially to me. Now he will mean much more to you too, because he is not only a servant but also your brother in Christ.

If I am really your friend, give him the same welcome you would give to me if I were the one who was coming. If he has harmed you in any way or stolen anything from you, charge me for it. I will pay it back (I, Paul, personally guarantee this by writing it here with my own hand). . . .

I've written you this letter because I am positive that you will do what I ask and even more!

Please keep a guest room ready for me, for I am hoping that God will answer your prayers and let me come to you soon.

Epaphras my fellow prisoner, who is also here for preaching Christ Jesus, sends you his greetings. So do Mark, Aristarchus, Demas and Luke, my fellow workers. The blessings of our Lord Jesus Christ be upon your spirit.

Paul

THE BOOK OF PHILEMON, TLB

Humble thyself in all things.

THOMAS À KEMPIS
fifteenth-century German Christian author

Meet the Dream Weavers

With God, nobody's hopeless.

Franklin Graham

Stubborn, self-willed, and hardheaded, Franklin was a headache for his big sisters and a handful for his parents, Ruth and Billy Graham. The dream of Franklin's very public life was to carve out for himself his own identity. He didn't want to be a carbon copy of his father. As he grew, he fought harder, and his frustration mounted. He became a rebel, a prodigal son.

Franklin was born in 1952. Folks sent their best wishes and hoped that he would become a "little preacher" following in his daddy's footsteps to the pulpit. It is often difficult for a famous person's child to carve out a niche. As much as he loved his father, Franklin fought tidal waves of expectations.

He didn't do well in school and often got into fights. Usually, he claimed to be trying to protect some smaller or helpless child from school bullies. Nonetheless, he was constantly in trouble. His poor grades and fighting worried his parents, so they decided to send him off to a private Christian school. There he balked at the regimentation and loss of privacy. He was mortified to be required to repeat the eighth grade. He found himself homesick for his family and for their home and the outdoors.

It wasn't until Franklin was grown that he was able to come to grips with himself. He realized how much people cared about him and that his parents only wanted him to be free from his anger and resentment. He turned from his sinful lifestyle and committed his life to God. Then he was able to finally be comfortable with being a Graham.

Franklin followed his passion for serving God in his own way—by helping people suffering in crisis and poverty worldwide. His hope is to fulfill the scripture in Matthew 25:35–36, and 40 (NASB), "I was hungry, and you gave Me something to eat; I was thirsty, and you gave Me something to drink; I was a stranger, and you invited Me in; naked, and you clothed Me; I was sick, and you visited Me; I was in prison, and you came to Me. . . . To the extent that you did it to one of these brothers of Mine, even the least of them, you did it to Me."

Franklin leads Samaritan's Purse, a charitable organization that provides help to people all over the globe who have been victims of earthquakes, floods, hurricanes, and other natural disasters. He sends crews in with food, water, clothing, medical supplies, and whatever is needed. One of his programs gathers and sends shoeboxes of gifts to poverty-stricken children in third-world countries at Christmastime.

Mr. Graham must thrill to think of poverty-stricken children opening a Christmas shoebox. He must find great comfort in helping the helpless and bringing hope to the hopeless and joy to breaking hearts. He began his life fighting for what he wanted most but has found happiness and fulfillment by fighting for those things that matter most to God.

My child, listen to me and do as I say,
and you will have a long, good life.
I will teach you wisdom's ways
and lead you in straight paths.
When you walk, you won't be held back;
when you run, you won't stumble.

PROVERBS 4:10–12 NLT

139

THE POWER OF POTENTIAL

Do you have ideas about what you think matters to God? Make a list of those things. When you are finished, read through the gospel of John in a "red-letter" edition of the Bible, looking for all the verses in red type. These indicate the words of Jesus. See how your list measures up to what Jesus had to say.

No, O people, the LORD has told you what is good, and this is what he requires of you: to do what is right, to love mercy, and to walk humbly with your God.

MICAH 6:8 NLT

HONESTY

Fair, just, truthful, morally upright

To be honest, as this world goes, is to be one man picked out of ten thousand.
WILLIAM SHAKESPEARE
sixteenth-century English dramatist and poet

Make yourself a seller when you are buying, and a buyer when you are selling, and then you will sell and buy justly.
SAINT FRANCIS DE SALES
seventeenth-century bishop of Geneva and Roman Catholic saint

Honesty has a beautiful and refreshing simplicity about it. No ulterior motives. No hidden meanings. An absence of hypocrisy, duplicity, political games, and verbal superficiality. As honesty and real integrity characterize our lives, there will be no need to manipulate others.
CHARLES R. SWINDOLL
twentieth-century author and theologian

An honest man's the noblest work of God.
ALEXANDER POPE
eighteenth-century English poet

Honesty is the best policy.
RICHARD WHATELY
nineteenth-century theologian, logician, and social reformer

WISDOM SPEAKS

It feels like my friends are changing. One of them is so ambitious. Everything she does is focused on making money and getting ahead in the world. Another friend is about to get married. Her whole vocabulary is wedding jargon. A third wants to be a star. He can act and sing, but he can't seem to relate to the rest of us. I am not focused like they are. What should I strive for?

Seek ye first the kingdom of God and his righteousness, and all these things shall be added unto you.
MATTHEW 6:33 KJV

Most of the trouble in the world is caused by people wanting to be important.
T. S. ELIOT
twentieth-century British poet and critic

Your talent is God's gift to you. What you do with it is your gift back to God.
LEO BUSCAGLIA
popular American author, educator, and lecturer

Ask yourself these three rational questions: (1) Where am I? (2) Where do I want to be? and (3) How do I know I am getting there?
AUTHOR UNKNOWN

My friends say they will do anything to get ahead, but I don't feel right about that. Am I overreacting?

The fruit of the Spirit is not push, drive, climb, grasp, and trample. Don't let the rat-racing world keep you on its treadmill. There is a legitimate place for blood, sweat, and tears, but it should have its roots in the call of God, not in the desire to get ahead. Life is more than a climb to the top of the heap.

RICHARD J. FOSTER
twentieth-century American religious writer

Live as you will wish to have lived when you are dying.

CHRISTIAN FÜRCHTEGOTT GELLERT
eighteenth-century German poet

Ambition destroys its possessor.

TALMUD
collection of ancient rabbinic writings on Jewish law and tradition

Our business in life is not to get ahead of others, but to get ahead of ourselves—to break our own records, to outstrip our yesterday by our today, to do our work with more force than ever before.

STEWARD B. JOHNSON
American businessman

SAY YES TO GOD'S PURPOSE AND PLAN FOR YOUR LIFE

Connecting with the
Creator of the Universe

Before me, even as behind,
God is, and all is well.

JOHN GREENLEAF WHITTIER
nineteenth-century American poet

Commit your work to the Lord,
then it will succeed.

PROVERBS 16:3 TLB

The Right Job for Me!

Jean Wensink

In 1982 I graduated from college with a degree in elementary education and was ready to take the classroom by storm. I was praying to land a job by the end of the summer so that I could begin the school year teaching. But where would the Lord lead me?

After sending out one hundred letters and résumés, I received a few calls for interviews. I wasn't too fussy about location or even grade level; I just wanted to begin my career. Each time I interviewed, I would get my hopes up, envisioning where I would start my new life, set up my apartment, and live an adult lifestyle. But after each rejection I was dejected and wondered if I would ever get a job. I began to question my career choice, planned for a future without teaching, and wondered how God would use me. I was compelled to put my life in God's hands and be willing to go wherever He led me.

I continued to apply for anything I was qualified for, confident that God would reveal His plan for my life. After all, my future was in His hands. At the end of August, I was called to interview at a small technical college. I would be teaching computers and math to adults. Perhaps this was where I was needed. I was qualified for the job.

As I was waiting to hear their decision, a tiny school district called me to interview the very next day. One of their teachers had unexpectedly broken her contract, and they needed a new teacher immediately because school was starting in less than a week. Without even knowing where the district was located, I said of course I could come for the interview and took down directions. Early the next morning, I got dressed in my interviewing outfit, thinking that this was probably my last chance for a job because schools would be starting soon. I said a prayer and asked for God's leading, safe travel, and, of course, His calming assurance.

The position was everything I had hoped for. I would be teaching first grade at a small rural school. The school was spacious, quaint, and built next to a church. It seemed perfect for me, but would the interviewing team feel the same way? As I drove the ninety minutes home, I prayed that an answer would be revealed. Which job was right for me, the technical college or the elementary-school position? How would I decide if I had to choose between the two? What if I wasn't offered either job?

I pulled my old car into the driveway, ran into the kitchen, and greeted my mom and dad with a "Hi, I'm home!" Just then the phone rang. It was the school district calling, and they offered me the first-grade position. I would start the very next day! I eagerly accepted, hung up the phone, and let out a whoop that was heard throughout the house. I had landed a job!

During my dancing and jumping around, my mom brought in the mail, and I noticed an important-looking letter addressed to me in the batch. It was from the technical college, offering me the position of adult math and computer teacher. There was quite a difference between the two positions—especially in terms of salary. That evening I wrote a letter to turn down the position teaching adults, even though it seemed to be the better of the two offers.

Now, twenty-four years later, I am still teaching in the same district. I still love teaching young children and know that it is my calling. Every time I try to spread my wings and try my hand at administration or teaching college, the Lord nudges me back to the classroom. He has His ways of putting people where He wants them in order to do His work. We just have to be open and listen to His voice.[12]

From *Running Barefoot on Holy Ground*

Jeanne Gowen Dennis
American writer

Limited though it is, our awareness of God's supreme holiness must inspire us to humility. As our Almighty God, Creator, and Savior, He has a right to demand anything of us. We owe Him everything. So when we stand in the presence of God to worship Him, shouldn't we bare our feet, at least in spirit, and take off our self-righteousness, self-sufficiency, and pride as we acknowledge our sinfulness and vulnerability? Shouldn't we offer Him the ultimate honor and respect? Let us humble ourselves before Him, for truly, when we are in His presence, we stand on holy ground.[13]

THE POWER OF POTENTIAL

Meditate on God's holiness. How do you want to respond?

The chief end of man is to glorify God and enjoy Him forever.

THE SHORTER CATECHISM

GOD'S WILL

Understand and follow your greatest purpose

*To will the will of God in himself and for himself
and concerning himself is the highest possible
condition of a man.*

GEORGE MACDONALD
nineteenth-century Scottish novelist and poet

The center of God's will is our only safety.

BETSIE TEN BOOM
Dutch Christian Holocaust victim

*There are no disappointments to those whose wills are
buried in the will of God.*

FREDERICK WILLIAM FABER
nineteenth-century devotional and hymn writer

In his will is our peace.

DANTE ALIGHIERI
fourteenth-century Italian author and poet

*The main thing in this world is not being
sure what God's will is, but seeking it
sincerely, and following what we do
understand of it. The only possible answer
to the destiny of man is to seek without
respite to fulfill God's purpose.*

PAUL TOURNIER
twentieth-century Swiss physician

Everyone who breathes, high and low, educated and ignorant, young and old, man and woman, has a mission, has a work. We are not sent into this world for nothing; we are not born at random; we are not here, that we may go to bed at night, and get up in the morning, toil for our bread, eat and drink, laugh and joke, sin when we have a mind, and reform when we are tired of sinning, rear a family and die. God sees every one of us; He creates every soul . . . for a purpose.

JOHN HENRY NEWMAN
nineteenth-century English cardinal and theologian

Dear brothers,
Is your life full of difficulties and temptations? Then be happy, for when the way is rough, your patience has a chance to grow. So let it grow, and don't try to squirm out of your problems. For when your patience is finally in full bloom, then you will be ready for anything, strong in character, full and complete.

If you want to know what God wants you to do, ask Him, and He will gladly tell you, for He is always ready to give a bountiful supply of wisdom to all who ask Him; He will not resent it. But when you ask Him, be sure that you really expect Him to tell you, for a doubtful mind will be as unsettled as a wave of the sea that is driven and tossed by the wind; . . . Whatever is good and perfect comes to us from God, the Creator of all light, and He shines forever without change or shadow.

JAMES 1:2–6, 17 TLB

My Dream Job It Wasn't!

LeAnn Campbell

My childhood dream? I don't remember having one. But I knew what I wanted by the time I finished high school. I had decided to work my way through college, earn a teaching degree, and teach kindergarten the rest of my life.

Marriage did not figure into the dream because I had not met anyone special. But then it happened. My college roommate set me up on a blind date with her future husband's brother. We fell in love and married after my second year of college.

For twenty years, I forgot about teaching. Then our local school district hired me as assistant kindergarten teacher. That revived my old dream. With my husband's encouragement (and a student loan and a scholarship for mature women), I returned to college just two weeks before my fortieth birthday.

I did it! At the age of forty-two, I took my place in line with the other graduates and received my college degree. Now I was ready to start teaching five-year-olds in a kindergarten class. With résumés in hand, I made the rounds of area schools for interviews.

"Sorry," the first superintendent said. "We don't have any vacancies." At every school I heard the same words.

Now what? Here I was ready to teach, and nobody needed me.

"The Developmental Center needs a teacher," a friend said. "Why don't you go by for a visit?" The Center served children with developmental disabilities—not what I wanted, but to please her I went.

At the center I experienced culture shock, for I did not know such a classroom existed in our town. It was not even part of the school system—just a rented room in an otherwise vacant building.

Those children needed a teacher trained to work with severe disabilities. They didn't need me. I would stay until noon, but no longer. However, God had insight that I lacked. By noon those children had won me over. I soon signed a contract to teach them and enrolled in night classes for the necessary special-education courses.

The children and youth (up to age twenty-one) needed basic skills for daily living. Instead of blackboards and books, my teaching supplies included educational toys for therapy, sing-along tapes for stimulation, and plenty of TLC (tender loving care).

The other staff members and I loved children and wanted to help these develop their limited abilities. We took them for their first horseback rides. We coached Roger to get off the floor and into his chair without assistance. When he succeeded, he rewarded us with a happy smile.

Our children needed to learn to play. The center's backyard had trees, and in the fall, we taught the children to run and jump into piles of leaves. What fun for all of us! In wintertime, we played in the snow and made snow ice cream.

When Jim, a teenager, asked how bread got brown on top, we let him find out for himself. Following a pictorial recipe on poster board, Jim made bread. Fascinated, he watched through the glass in the oven door as the bread baked and saw the crust turn a golden brown.

How I loved that job! But perfect jobs do not always last. After four years, circumstances changed. Most of the children lived in a group home, and problems developed that caused the state agency to place them in other facilities.

I went job hunting again. Although I still loved kindergarten children, by this time I had a special love for students with special needs.

I approached the superintendent of our local school district and heard the same words I'd heard four years earlier. "We don't have any openings." But this time he went one step further. Picking up a paper from his desk, he explained that the state Department of Education had just granted approval for a new program in our school district. The job was for a resource teacher to help high-school students who had learning disabilities in a vocational-technical school.

"Are you interested?" he asked.

I said yes. Once again, God had intervened and led me to the right job.

In the vocational-technical school, my students explored different types of work and learned to fill out job applications. I prepared them for driving tests, helped health-occupations students learn to make beds so they could become nurses' aides, and guided carpentry students in making correct measurements.

Sometimes perfect jobs do last. That one did, and I stayed until it was time to retire.

I didn't choose special education for myself, but I believe with all my heart that God chose it for me. I'm thankful for the day I walked into a roomful of developmentally disabled students. It was the beginning of a rewarding career—one that was part of God's best plan and purpose for my life.

My dream of teaching kindergarten children? I didn't lose it. Although I never taught the little ones in public school, they have been my Sunday-school students for more than forty years. I had the best of both worlds—five-year-olds in church every Sunday and teenagers with special needs Monday through Friday. Thank You, Lord![14]

Remember this. When people choose to withdraw far from a fire, the fire continues to give warmth, but they grow cold. When people choose to withdraw far from light, the light continues to be bright in itself but they are in darkness. This is also the case when people withdraw from God.

SAINT AUGUSTINE
fifth-century Catholic saint

The Beatitudes

Blessed are the poor in spirit, for theirs is the kingdom of heaven.
Blessed are those who mourn, for they will be comforted.
Blessed are the meek, for they will inherit the earth.
Blessed are those who hunger and thirst for righteousness,
for they will be filled.
Blessed are the merciful, for they will be shown mercy.
Blessed are the pure in heart, for they will see God.
Blessed are the peacemakers, for they will be called sons of God.
Blessed are those who are persecuted because of righteousness,
for theirs is the kingdom of heaven.

MATTHEW 5:3–10

1984 Commencement Address

Iona College in New Rochelle, New York

Mario Cuomo
fifty-second governor of New York state

How simple it seems now. We thought the Sermon on the Mount was a nice allegory and nothing more. What we didn't understand until we got to be a little older was that it was the whole answer, the whole truth. That the way—the only way—to succeed and to be happy is to learn those rules so basic that a shepherd's son could teach them to an ignorant flock without notes or formula.

We carried Saint Francis's prayer in our wallets for years and never learned to live the message.

Do we have the right now to tell them that when Saint Francis begged the Lord to teach him to want to console instead of seeking to be consoled—to teach him to want to love instead of desiring to be loved—that he was really being intensely selfish? Because he knew the only way to be fulfilled and pleased and happy was to give instead of trying to get.

We have for a full lifetime taught our children to be go-getters. Can we now say to them that if they want to be happy they must be go-givers?

Lord, What Is Your Plan for Me?

Linda Myers-Sowell

As I walked to the platform to receive my high-school graduation diploma, I was shaking with fear. My fear was not from being on the platform. My fear was from not knowing what I was going to do on Monday morning. No job, no plans—it seemed as if my life was about to come to a standstill.

All my friends had applied and been accepted to the local community college. At eighteen years of age, I wasn't sure I wanted to go to college even if there were money available. If I did go to college, what would I study? I had been praying every night for a long time that God would help me know what I should do after high school. I was being raised by a single mother making minimum wage. I felt that I needed to get a job to help my mother with the necessities of raising my sister and me. We had come close to losing our home a few times in the previous two years when my mother didn't have enough money to make the house payment. If I could get a job, my mother wouldn't have to worry about losing our house.

The next week I went around town and filled out applications. My only past job experience was babysitting. In high school I had taken all the available secretarial classes, and my typing speed was quite good. I felt sure that someone would want an eager-to-work high-school graduate. After many applications and very few interviews, I was hired as a part-time office assistant. I didn't have a car, and I didn't know how I would get to work. My mother drove me to work very early in the morning, and I waited for the office to open. I walked home after work.

One Sunday a deacon at our church asked my mother what I was going to do since I had finished high school. My mother told him what I was doing, and the deacon was surprised that I wasn't going to college. He later took me aside and asked if I wanted to go to our church-sponsored college in another town. I told him I might be interested, but we did not have any money to pay for community college—much less a private college. In a few days I received an application in the mail for the private college and financial assistance. I quickly completed the forms and enclosed a check in the envelope for the fees to process the application.

Every free moment, I prayed, asking God if attending the private church college was His plan for me. The thought of living on a college campus and attending school with other Christians seemed too good to be possible for me. I told myself, *Don't get your hopes up. How could you ever have the money to go there?* Several weeks went by, and I had not heard anything from the college. I became a little depressed. Summer was coming to an end, and my friends had completed their plans and registration for the community college. Every day I asked God and myself, *What am I supposed to do?*

Then a letter came from the college. I thought, *Well, at least they sent me a letter, even if it is impossible for me to attend.* When I read the letter, I found that I had been accepted by the college, I had a place in the dorm, and a part-time job on campus. All I needed was for my mother to cosign on a loan for my first semester. Asking my mother to cosign was very difficult for me, as I didn't want to put more responsibility on her. I was also feeling that I shouldn't be leaving her and my sister. When I showed my mother the letter from the college, she smiled. "This is what I was hoping and praying for, Linda. I will be happy to cosign the loan." I let out a little scream and said a quiet *thank you* to God.

Two weeks later, my mother drove me to the college to get settled in my dorm room.

My grandmother had given me my first suitcase and my mother gave me a few dollars for spending money until I started my new job. It didn't matter to me that I would still be wearing the same clothes from high school. God had led me here, and I knew that He would provide what I needed. Looking back, I grew so much in my spiritual walk in college, but it still would be several years before I really knew what my life's "calling" would be.[15]

THE POWER OF POTENTIAL

How has God shown you His will in the past? How will you discover it in the future?

I am satisfied that when the Almighty wants me to do or not to do any particular thing, He finds a way of letting me know.
ABRAHAM LINCOLN
sixteenth U.S. president

Prayer

Henry van Dyke

twentieth-century American pastor and educator

Lord, the newness of this day
Calls me to an untried way:
Let me gladly take the road,
Give me strength to bear my load,
Thou my guide and helper be—
I will travel through with Thee.

For He will not be false to you, I say
If all your heart on Him you wholly lay.
GEOFFREY CHAUCER
fourteenth-century English poet

Search me, O God, and know my heart; test my thoughts.
Point out anything you find in me that makes you sad,
and lead me along the path of everlasting life.
PSALM 139:23–24 TLB

Meet the Dream Weavers

*My artwork is an attempt to honor
the creator for His blessings.*

Buck Taylor

Maybe you knew him as "Newly." Taylor played the part of
the deputy marshal of Dodge City, Newly O'Brien, for eight years
(1967–1975) on the long-running television drama *Gunsmoke*.
William Clarence Taylor's father was actor Dub Taylor, who
appeared in many Hollywood movies and later in the popular
series *Maverick*. Taylor appeared in more than one hundred movies
besides his television acting and still takes acting parts occasionally.

Taylor went into the movies after college as a stunt man and
later took some bit parts on *Gunsmoke* until he landed the role of
deputy marshal, but his real passion was art. Taylor loved painting
and studied art at the University of Southern California in Los
Angeles. He is now a renowned artist, noted for his Western
artwork of cowboys and horses, after the style of Remington. One
of his favorite works is a portrait of his friend James Arness, who
starred in *Gunsmoke* for many years. Arness was a hero and role
model for Taylor.

You might be amused if you saw him today. Taylor dresses like
a cowboy, complete with white hat, Western neckerchief, vest, and
boots. His bushy mustache suits him well and can't begin to hide
his friendly smile. Taylor spends seven weeks each year in Branson,
Missouri, at Silver Dollar City theme park where he displays and
sells his art and meets visitors in a barn art gallery.

Though he struggled with his faith in God when he lost his son
Adam in a motorcycle accident, his wife, Goldie, supported him
and helped him cling to his faith through the grieving process. He

found that his faith was strengthened despite the inexplicable loss of his precious son.

Taylor made a good living for many years in the movies and on television, but in 1990, he decided to finally get serious about his passion for painting. Most of his works are watercolors with the Western theme. For Taylor the dream had to ride double for many years, but his love for a paintbrush and canvas finally has been realized. Never give up on a dream—especially one that God puts in your heart.

If the LORD delights in a man's way, he makes his steps firm; though he stumble, he will not fall, for the LORD upholds him with his hand.
PSALM 37:23–24

O Lord, I give myself to thee, I trust thee wholly. Thou art wiser than I,—more loving to me than I myself. Deign to fulfill thy high purposes in me whatever they be,—work in and through me. I am born to serve thee, to be thine, to be thy instrument. I ask not to see,—I ask not to know,—I ask simply to be used. Amen.

JOHN HENRY NEWMAN
nineteenth-century English cardinal and theologian

Bloom

Taprina Milburn

I absolutely love the big city. Everything about the hustle and bustle of urban America—the elbow-to-elbow crowds, the smell of hot dogs cooking in the vendors' carts, taxis sounding their horns, and a Starbucks on every corner.

The seemingly endless opportunities of a big city pulled at me as a college student.

My journalism degree would take me to all the exciting places I wanted to experience, I believed. Maybe I'd have a much-sought-after position working for a large daily newspaper covering politics, crime, or even Wall Street. The city would become *my* city.

I had dreams, and, believe me, I wasn't shy about letting God in on those plans.

The president of the Christian university I attended delivered a speech near the end of my senior year and told the students in the crowd, "Bloom where God plants you." I'd heard variations of that charge many times before, but I wrote it in my notebook that morning.

You see, by then I knew I wasn't leaving my small town after graduation. I had since married. My husband had an established career in the town where we lived and where I was finishing up my degree.

God had brought my husband to me, there is no doubt, but I felt let down. Wasn't God listening to me when I let Him in on my plans? I held regret in my heart that I wouldn't live out my dream of working and living in a large city.

Sometimes regret will prevent blooming.

I landed a job as a reporter in a rural community that neighbors my town. Instead of riding the subway to cover an important political meeting, one of my first assignments was driving my car across a field to take a picture of a farmer and his prize-winning cantaloupe. I've indeed reported on politics, sitting in on town-council meetings that went long into the night. And the closest assignments I've had to the nation's financial district were articles about a school-bond issue and a comparison piece on the rising cost of cable television.

Not so glamorous, I'll admit.

There was a part of me that felt that if I could only convince my husband to leave our town, I'd have him sold on my big-city dream too. That's when my *real* life and *real* career would begin. But my efforts led nowhere. As my husband bloomed and thrived in our town, I chose to remain dormant. He seemed to know something that I didn't.

When you live as if you're headed somewhere else, someplace better than where you are, you don't drop roots. Nor do you relax. Like a shy, nervous kid, you sort of hang back in the shadows and don't risk getting attached to people or places. This isn't the way to live life.

I'm grateful for my husband's steady example—not to mention stubbornness—because along the way I began to love where I was and saw the blessings in the work I was doing right in my own town. I believe the transition had a lot to do with my learning to listen to *God's* plan for my life rather than acting like a petulant child demanding that He listen to me instead.

Years after that first newspaper job, I bought a brightly colored, whimsical poster that says, "Bloom Where You Are Planted." It hangs on my office wall today and reminds me of what I would have missed if I'd left our town.

God didn't have plans for me to live and work in a big city. Instead He has encouraged me to take root and bloom in a community where I have endless opportunities to listen to and write about the lives of people who sit next to me in church on Sunday or who lead my children in after-school activities (people who don't have a two-hour commute to and from work).

I've since written articles about teen rodeo queens, parents of handicapped children, volunteer firemen, and high-school valedictorians, to name only a few. My life is richer for having heard others' stories of faith and struggles as well as tales of their hopes and dreams—some achieved, but many redirected by God's guiding hand.[16]

THE POWER OF POTENTIAL

Does the grass look greener elsewhere? Where does God want you to bloom?

Faith is required of thee, and a sincere life, not loftiness of intellect, nor deepness in the mysteries of God.

THOMAS À KEMPIS
fifteenth-century German Christian author

Words from Woodrow Wilson

twenty-eighth U.S. president

The Bible is the Word of Life. I beg you will read it and find this out for yourself—read, not little snatches here and there, but long passages that will really be the road to the heart of it.

You will not only find it full of real men and women, but also of things you have wondered about and been troubled about all your life, as men have been always, and the more you read, the more will it become plain to you what things are worthwhile and what are not; what things make men happy—loyalty, right dealing, speaking the truth, readiness to give everything for what they think their duty, and, most of all, the wish that they may have the real approval of the Christ, who gave everything for them; and the things that are guaranteed to make men unhappy—selfishness, cowardice, greed, and everything that is low and mean.

When you have read the Bible, you will know that it is the Word of God, because you will have found it the key to your own heart, your own happiness, and your own duty.

And in life, in death, in dark and light,
All are in God's care;
Sound the black abyss, pierce the deep of night,
And he is there!

JOHN GREENLEAF WHITTIER
nineteenth-century American poet

GOD'S WILL

Questions to Ponder

★ If you are not following God, what else are you doing?

★ If God only wants what's best for you, why are you holding Him back?

★ If God has your best interest in mind, why are you fighting Him?

★ Your pursuit of God is eternal. What else in life lasts forever?

★ People regret a lot of things when they are dying, but how many people on their deathbeds wish they hadn't spent so much time pursuing God?

They say you can't take it with you, but they're wrong. You can take your relationship with God with you to the grave and beyond.
SHEILA SEIFERT
American writer

From *Running Barefoot on Holy Ground*

Jeanne Gowen Dennis
American writer

Instead of judging our lives by the little details that might look like flaws up close, we can see more clearly after time has passed. The distance of time allows us to appreciate His exquisite technique from a vantage point that allows us to comprehend the heart of the Artist. Then we can recognize the beauty produced by splashes of colorful blessings contrasted with flat sections of waiting. We can even appreciate the value of ugly splotches of pain, which add the depth of shadow and help define and brighten our times of joy.

The Artist is fashioning each one of His children into a masterpiece, but as viewers of His work, we usually stand too close. Therefore, we sometimes notice the frame instead of the art—the circumstances in lieu of the results, or the areas of shadow instead of the overall picture. Only He can heal our blindness by pulling us back, back, back until we can see more clearly. We just have to let Him lead us to that place of understanding.[17]

> When God contemplates some great work, He begins it by the hand of some poor, weak, human creature, to whom He afterwards gives aid, so that the enemies who seek to obstruct it are overcome.
>
> **MARTIN LUTHER**
> *sixteenth-century German Reformation leader*

Man doth what he can, and God what He will.

JOHN CLARKE
former Supreme Court justice

Many are the plans in a man's heart, but it is the LORD's purpose that prevails.

PROVERBS 19:21

There is no action so slight, nor so mean, but it may be done to a great purpose, and ennobled therefore; nor is any purpose so great but that slight actions may help it, and may be so done as to help it much.

JOHN RUSKIN
most influential English critic of the 1800s

Man thinks; God directs.

ALCUIN
eighth-century theologian and scholar

God shall be my hope, my stay, my guide and lantern to my feet.

WILLIAM SHAKESPEARE
sixteenth-century English dramatist and poet

Meet the Dream Weavers

*No limit can be placed on what can
be achieved when you accept God
as your partner.*

R. G. LeTourneau

He stopped for a quick nap on an old army cot pushed against
the side of one windowless wall when he had exhausted himself
working on another of his enormous ideas. Blueprints, scraps of
paper covered with drawings and illegible writing, half a dozen
books, a couple of spiral notebooks, and pencils were piled high on
his small, metal desk. A dorm fridge held simple snacks for late-
night sustenance.

The engineering genius R. G. LeTourneau kept an office that
was not what you'd expect of the CEO of a large corporation,
especially considering his factories built more than 50 percent of
the earth-moving equipment used in World War II.

LeTourneau dropped out of school when he was fourteen and
went to work in Portland, Oregon, at an ironwork, shoveling sand
and dirt. He was a large man, tough, hardened, stubborn, and
willful by nature. When he grew up enough to realize his need for
God, he decided to change.

He became a machinery manufacturer and inventor, working
during the economic hardships of the thirties and against a public
who could not share the passion that grew in his heart to build
gigantic equipment—monstrous machines for megajobs, to clear
land for farms to feed hungry people across the world.

Many of his ideas, though they seemed simple in his eyes, were
difficult to manufacture. Few facilities were designed for such
huge parts and equipment. LeTourneau fought to build each new

machine he imagined and designed. The bulldozer, road graders, tree crushers, as well as jungle-clearing, bridge-building, and road-building equipment rolled out of huge, dome-shaped factories in Texas—the state where everything is big!

Early on, he made a decision that was as big and visionary as any of his inventions. He turned the tables on the tithe. Instead of giving 10 percent of his income to God and keeping 90, he gave 90 and kept 10. The result? He soon became a multimillionaire.

R. G. LeTourneau referred to himself as "a hick from the backwoods of Duluth." He never made it into high school, yet he started a technical school in Longview, Texas, that is today a thriving university, named after him. Students there combine his two passions—sharing God's love and engineering.

It is said of LeTourneau: "In our high-tech age, machines—really big machines that push and pull, lift and move—are not too popular anymore. However, without the kinds of machines he dreamed of . . . the technological age we are in now might never have happened at all."

Remember this: Whoever sows sparingly will also reap sparingly, and whoever sows generously will also reap generously.

2 Corinthians 9:6

THE POWER OF POTENTIAL

Determine to invest in God's kingdom. Decide what percentage of your income you want to invest and where you wish to give. In addition to your church, there are many charities and worthy causes where you can honor God with your finances.

I commit you to God and to the word of his grace, which can build you up and give you an inheritance among all those who are sanctified.
ACTS 20:32

When one door of happiness closes, another opens; but often we look so long at the closed door that we do not see the one which has been opened for us.
HELEN KELLER
twentieth-century American deafblind lecturer and author

ON YOUR OWN

Tips for Feeding Your Soul

Graduation often means a change of location. Those family and friends you counted on and the church you felt comfortable in may be unavailable to you. If that happens, you will need to know how to nourish your soul in a strange and new place. Consider these suggestions.

☐ **More than ever, prayer is your lifeline.** Talk to God often about everything you are encountering. Thank Him for the good things, and pour out your heart to Him concerning your challenges. You couldn't ask for a better friend.

☐ **Read your Bible.** More than just a "good book," the Bible is God's love letter to you. It tells you who you are and why you are here. In addition, it provides a source of comfort and sound advice for anything you might encounter.

☐ **Build strong relationships with other Christians.** Look for Bible-study groups, especially those for your age group. Those sponsored by churches provide a level of safety and accountability.

☐ **Read faith-inspiring books.** Find out where the Christian bookstores are in town and visit them often.

☐ **Join a church.** Choose carefully, and base your decision on things like Bible-based teaching, good worship, other parishioners your age, and a variety of activities that interest you.

Stronger Than You Think

Brenna Fay Rhodes

I tried to hold back the tears, but it was no use. They snuck down my cheeks before I even made it into the kitchen.

Mom was standing at the window with her back to me, looking out. "Isn't it gorgeous today? My redbud tree is just one solid bloom, and the amaryllis are stunning," she said. She turned toward me, and her smile faded. "Hey, what's the matter? What is it, honey?"

I didn't even answer but handed the stack of mail to her and flopped down at the table. She read the open letter on top, then asked, "So, what's the problem?" She poured herself a cup of coffee and stood beside me.

My thoughts came out in a rush. "I just can't believe it, Mom. I worked my hardest. I paid for tutors, met with study groups. I studied constantly. I still failed. An F! I can't believe I have an F in calculus," I said.

Mom hugged me and said, "I'm sorry. That stinks to work so hard and not be successful. I'm really sorry." She handed me a tissue and sat down at the table.

I sniffed and blew my nose. "This is going to kill my grade point average. I'll lose my scholarships and probably never get another university grant. What if I lose my student internship?" I said. "Then I won't get the job I want, because no one is going to hire a complete failure. I'm not strong enough to keep working like this and still fail. It's just too hard. I'll never get over this. Never."

Mom handed me another tissue. She added cream to her coffee and stirred slowly as she spoke. "Your grandmother Feaster studied to be a teacher when no one believed in her or her dreams. No one helped her. The college administration didn't really want her there because she was a woman. Her parents thought she was crazy and refused to help her, so she paid her own way. Through hard work and determination she earned the respect of her professors. She was one of the first women in Texas to earn her college degree. She persevered and got her diploma and went on to influence the lives of hundreds of students during her long teaching career. When I was a little girl, I knew that I'd grow up and get my degree and be a teacher, just like my mother. I figured if she could do it with the whole world against her, surely I could too. So I did." Mom straightened the blue placemat in front of her and smiled at me. "You come from tough stock, honey. You can do this."

I stared into space and pictured my grandmother as a young woman. In old photographs, she looks a lot like me.

Mom put her hand on top of mine and squeezed. "I guarantee you this: ten years from now, you won't even remember today," she said. "Life goes on, and what seems insurmountable today is really just a blip on the radar screen of your life. Go ahead and feel disappointed today. Then get over it. God has big plans for your life. Pick yourself up, dust yourself off, and get back in the game. You, my dear, are stronger than you think."

She was right, as mothers usually are. None of the disasters I predicted came true after that F on my grade report. I went on to graduate with honors and enjoy a fulfilling career. No one ever asks to see my calculus grade from college. I've experienced hundreds of days filled with incredible joy and survived several days filled with tragic grief. Life is more complicated and sweeter and fuller now than I ever could have imagined that warm spring day at the kitchen table when I was a junior in college staring at my first bad grade on university letterhead.

But Mom was wrong about one thing: more than ten years later, I do remember that day and that failing grade, with clarity. I will never forget that day. That's the day I realized my grandmother paved the way for me to reach all my goals. She set an example of strength for me and for my children, and for their children. With my grandmother behind me and the Lord as my source, I am stronger than I thought.[18]

Obedience

Phoebe Cary

nineteenth-century American poet

If you're told to do a thing,
And mean to do it really,
Never let it be by halves;
Do it fully, freely!

Do not make a poor excuse,
Waiting, weak, unsteady;
All obedience worth the name
Must be prompt and ready.

*I come to the office each morning and
stay for long hours doing what has to be
done to the best of my ability. And when
you've done the best you can, you can't
do any better. So when I go to sleep I turn
everything over to the Lord and forget it.*

HARRY S. TRUMAN
thirty-third U.S. president

Decide on what you think is right, and stick to it.
GEORGE ELIOT
nineteenth-century British novelist

The LORD Almighty has purposed, and who can thwart him? His hand is stretched out, and who can turn it back?
ISAIAH 14:27

Trusting even when it appears you have been forsaken . . . believing that God's love is complete and that He is aware of your circumstances, even when your world seems to grind on as if setting its own direction . . . desiring only what God's hands have planned for you . . . this is genuine faith indeed.
GEORGE MACDONALD
nineteenth-century Scottish novelist and poet

It is the heart always that sees before the head can see.
THOMAS CARLYLE
nineteenth-century Scottish essayist and historian

Oftentimes I find myself hesitating to move forward with what I know is God's will for my life. Even though I am certain He would never ask me to do anything He has not equipped me to do, even though I know He will be with me every step of the way—still I find myself unable to walk into the unknown.

Do you find yourself in such a position? Do you want desperately to step into God's perfect will, but you are fearful of what lies ahead? You don't know me, and I don't know you. We may not even be living at the same time in history. But our struggles are the same. Christians throughout the centuries have felt as we feel right now. So, let's draw courage from each other, from the commonality of our desire to please our heavenly Father and the acknowledgement of our humanity. Together, let's let go of our fears and insecurities and let God take us to new places of faith and fulfillment. How about it? I will if you will walk bravely into God's will.

REBECCA S. MCMILLAN
American writer

"I know the plans I have for you," declares the LORD, *"plans to prosper you and not to harm you, plans to give you hope and a future. Then you will call upon me and come and pray to me, and I will listen to you. You will seek me and find me when you seek me with all your heart."*
JEREMIAH 29:11–13

Unidirectional Showers

Matthew Kinne

Answered prayer can strike in the strangest places. For me, it happened in the shower. I had been struggling as a teacher at a small Christian school where I taught all subjects. Furthermore, this school contained "problem kids"; kids were sent there to "straighten them out." I wasn't doing well, and I wasn't passionate about my work. So one spring day as I vacationed in Florida at my grandparents' condo, God spoke to me—in the shower.

I had been praying, "God, what do You want me to do?" And He seemed to answer, *What do you want to do?* Halfheartedly, I answered "film school." I hadn't really seriously considered going to film school. It was more of a fantasy or a dream. But when I said those words to God, a peace like I hadn't known before came over me in a powerful way. I finished, "God, if this is from You, please guide me to the right school."

Following this prayer, I returned to Michigan. A friend suggested I look into Regent University in Virginia Beach. He studied psychology there, and he knew it had a good film program. I applied and was accepted!

Throughout my grad-school education, I doubted if I had made the right decision. Not being an undergrad communication major, I found classes more difficult than I had expected. I also worked my way through school to pay not only for my schooling but also room, board, car insurance, fuel, and other expenses. One semester, I didn't have enough money for tuition, so I just worked and watched films on my own dime and time.

Nearing graduation, I still had no clue what I was going to do with my future. I didn't really want to go to Hollywood, and I also found the production world quite arduous. Had I just wasted three years and thousands of dollars?

My answer came just one month before graduation day. I was doing temp work for CBN in their warehouse—one of the most unglamorous positions they had. On one particularly busy day, I was sweat drenched and tired. Yet I still had to report to the mandatory chapel services they held once a week. I showed up late to chapel and wound up sitting in the only available seat—right on the front row.

The chapel speaker that day was Dr. Ted Baehr, chairman of the Christian Film and Television Commission and founder of a movie magazine. He made a compelling argument on Christians in entertainment and the importance of complete content analysis, including worldview discussion, in writing movie reviews. I was enthralled and totally captured. His organization seemed like a perfect match for both my education and my strong faith.

After Dr. Baehr finished talking, he didn't walk away from the podium. He lingered for a while—mere feet in front of me. Nobody else was talking to him, so I approached him and thanked him for his speech. Then I asked him if he needed any help. I told him I was about to graduate from Regent's film program. To my surprise, he said he did indeed have a writer/editor position available and I should come down to Atlanta right away and have a formal interview with him.

The very next week, I drove in my old jalopy down to Atlanta and met Dr. Baehr and the rest of his staff. I talked with him in his book-filled office, and he offered me a job on the spot. We shook hands, and I drove back to Virginia Beach to graduate.

Graduation day came with lots of laughs, hugs, parties—and a little sadness. Many of my friends had no clue what they were going to do. Some had even told me they were going home to enter the family business. The day after graduation, I packed up what little belongings I had and drove down to Atlanta. The next day I started working as an associate editor for a movie magazine.

Today I am still a writer. I've authored a movie devotional book, and I do a weekly and daily radio program on what else—the movies! I also speak to church groups and schools on a Christian understanding of the movies. I write screenplays that some directors like.

I'm not rich, and I might never be. The big bucks belong to the Hollywood types, I guess. But I do have purpose and a fascinating job. I just attended my twentieth high-school reunion, and classmates told me they envied my job. I'm blessed and content that I've found God's purpose and plan for my life.[19]

Here is the conclusion of the matter: Fear God and keep His commandments, for this is the whole duty of man. For God will bring every deed into judgment, including every hidden thing, whether it is good or evil.

ECCLESIASTES 12:13–14

THE POWER OF POTENTIAL

Do you have an inner steadfastness? Put your future in God's hands and you, too, can move ahead with the dream God has placed in your life—patient, unruffled, unperturbed, and ultimately inscrutable. Break out of your stereotypes. Step out with confidence and courage, fully trusting in God's plan for your life. You are certain to become a champion!

Faithfulness in carrying out present duties is the best preparation for the future.

FRANÇOIS FÉNELON
seventeenth-century
French prelate and
writer

Be joyful always; pray continually; give thanks in all circumstances, for this is God's will for you in Christ Jesus.

1 THESSALONIANS 5:16–18

WISDOM SPEAKS

I have to make a decision between two things, both honoring God and both that I feel passionate about. How do I decide what is God's perfect will and purpose for me?

Do not conform any longer to the pattern of this world, but be transformed by the renewing of your mind. Then you will be able to test and approve what God's will is—his good, pleasing and perfect will.

ROMANS 12:2

When confronted with two courses of action, I jot down on a piece of paper all the arguments in favor of each one; then on the opposite side, I write the arguments against each one. Then by weighing the arguments, pro and con, and canceling them out, one against the other, I take the course indicated by what remains.

BENJAMIN FRANKLIN
eighteenth-century American statesman and philosopher

You are facing a dilemma; you are not quite sure which of two decisions to make. Apply the test of universality. Suppose your personal decision should become a universal custom, would it bring the world happiness or unhappiness?

JOSEPH R. SIZOO
clergyman and author

Will I ever know if the choice I made was the right choice?

Those who insist upon seeing with perfect clearness before they decide, never decide.

HENRY-FRÉDÉRIC AMIEL
nineteenth-century Swiss philosopher and poet

The disciple who is in the condition of abiding in Jesus is in the will of God, and his apparent free choices are God's foreordained decrees. Mysterious? Logically absurd? But a glorious truth to a saint.

OSWALD CHAMBERS
twentieth-century Scottish evangelist and devotional writer

No one learns to make right decisions without being free to make wrong ones.

KENNETH SOLLITT
American writer

I've heard that if you wait long enough for something, you will get it. Is that true?

Destiny is not a matter of chance, it is a matter of choice; it is not a thing to be waited for, it is a thing to be achieved.

WILLIAM JENNINGS BRYAN
twentieth-century American lawyer and politician

In any moment of decision the best thing you can do is the right thing, the next best thing is the wrong thing, and the worst thing you can do is nothing.

THEODORE ROOSEVELT
twenty-sixth U.S. president

Not to decide is to decide.

HARVEY COX
American educator and theologian

I have no answer for myself or thee,

Save that I learned beside my mother's knee;

"All is of God that is, and is to be;

And God is good." Let this suffice us still.

Resting in childlike trust upon His will.

JOHN GREENLEAF WHITTIER
nineteenth-century American poet

He made known to us the mystery of His will according to His good pleasure, which He purposed in Christ, to be put into effect when the times will have reached their fulfillment—to bring all things in heaven and on earth together under one head, even Christ.

In Him we were also chosen, having been predestined according to the plan of Him who works out everything in conformity with the purpose of His will, in order that we, who were the first to hope in Christ, might be for the praise of His glory.

EPHESIANS 1:9–12

Each man is Captain of his Soul,
And each man his own Crew,
But the Pilot knows the Unknown Seas,
And He will bring us through.
(from New Year's Day—Every Day)
JOHN OXENHAM
twentieth-century British journalist, novelist, and poet

The will of God—
Nothing more. Nothing less.
MOTTO IN G. CAMPBELL MORGAN'S STUDY
twentieth-century Bible teacher and evangelist

What God sends is better than what men ask for.
AUTHOR UNKNOWN

The world and its desires pass away,
but the man who does the will of God lives forever.
1 JOHN 2:17

O Will, that willest good alone,
Lead thou the way, thou guidest best;
A silent child, I follow on,
And trusting lean upon thy breast.
And if in gloom I see thee not,
I lean upon thy love unknown;
In me thy blessed will is wrought,
If I will nothing of my own.

Gerhard Tersteegen
eighteenth-century German religious writer

From "If"

Rudyard Kipling

If you can keep your head when all about you
Are losing theirs and blaming it on you;
If you can trust yourself when all men doubt you,
But make allowance for their doubting too;
If you can wait and not be tired by waiting,
Or, being lied about, don't deal in lies,
Or, being hated, don't give way to hating,
And yet don't look too good, nor talk too wise;

If you can dream—and not make dreams your master;
If you can think—and not make thoughts your aim;
If you can meet with triumph and disaster
And treat those two imposters just the same;
If you can bear to hear the truth you've spoken
Twisted by knaves to make a trap for fools,
Or watch the things you gave your life to broken,
And stoop and build 'em up with worn out tools;

If you can force your heart and nerve and sinew
To serve your turn long after they are gone,
And so hold on when there is nothing in you
Except the Will which says to them: "Hold on";
If you can fill the unforgiving minute
With sixty seconds' worth of distance run—
Yours is the Earth and everything that's in it,
And—which is more—you'll be a Man my son!

SAY YES TO PRACTICAL INSTRUCTION FOR YOUR FUTURE LIFE

Looking to
What Lies Ahead

Along the way you will stumble, and perhaps even fall; but that, too, is normal and to be expected. Get up, get back on your feet, chastened but wiser, and continue on down the road.

ARTHUR ASHE
twentieth-century American athlete

How can you hesitate? Risk!
Risk anything! Care no more for the
opinion of others, for those voices.
Do the hardest thing on earth for you.
Act for yourself. Face the truth.
KATHERINE MANSFIELD
twentieth-century New Zealand author

In the Midst of the Storm

Amy S. Bartlett
American writer

I don't like adversity. I prefer smooth sailing—calm waters and a safe harbor within sight. But distress and tribulation come to everyone. If I'm not careful, I will give into that feeling of dread—the thought that I am going under—I'm not going to make it through this.

But as a Christian, someone who has placed her trust in the Almighty One—I must not! The same One who slung the stars into space holds my hand. He knows my beginning and my end and He knew beforehand that this adversity would come.

So I must lean on His goodness and grace knowing that whatever my lot, He will sustain me and give me the wisdom I need. I must remember all the blessings of before that will come again. I *will* make it because *He* will not let me fall.

Life has no smooth road for any of us; and in the bracing atmosphere of a high aim the very roughness stimulates the climber to steadier steps, till the legend, "over steep ways to the stars," fulfills itself.

W. C. DOANE
bishop and hymn writer

THE POWER OF POTENTIAL

Are you facing adversity? How will it help to view your difficulty as a challenge that will help you grow?

Hold on; hold fast; hold out. Patience is genius.

COMTE DE BUFFON
eighteenth-century French naturalist

If you can't change your circumstances, change the way you respond to them.

AUTHOR UNKNOWN

Does the road wind uphill all the way?
Yes, to the very end.
Will the day's journey take the whole long day?
From morn to night, my friend.

CHRISTINA ROSSETTI
nineteenth-century English poet

MANAGING STRESS

Don't let stress manage you

★ Don't keep things inside. Find someone you can trust, and talk out the things that are bothering you.

★ Learn to be a listener for others, and build healthy relationships. Good relationships, especially laughter shared, relieve stress.

★ It's better to walk away from an angry situation than to escalate the problem. If you walk away, you can calm down and let the physical exercise of "walking away" release your pent-up anger.

★ If a problem seems impossible, sometimes it's better to go on to something else. Then after spending a few days away from it, the problem often doesn't seem as insurmountable.

★ A brisk walk or other physical activity is invaluable to release stress.

★ Take your mind off yourself, and help a friend. There's no better way to relieve stress than to help someone else.

★ Break large projects into smaller steps. Then after each step is completed, reward yourself and take a minibreak.

★ Don't be afraid you're going to fail. If you fail, you join the ranks of great inventors of our time. But when you fail, don't give up.

One Thing at a Time

Author Unknown

Work while you work,
Play while you play,
That is the way
To be cheerful and gay.

All that you do,
Do with your might;
Things done by halves
Are never done right.

One thing each time,
And that done well,
Is a very good rule
As many can tell.

Moments are useless,
Trifled away,
So work while you work,
And play while you play.

WORK

Taking care of business

★ *Every now and then, go away, have a little relaxation, for when you come back to your work, your judgment will be surer. Go some distance away because then the work appears smaller and more of it can be taken in at a glance and a lack of harmony and proportion is more readily seen.*

LEONARDO DA VINCI
fifteenth-century Italian painter, sculptor, architect, and engineer

★ *It is not only for what we do that we are held responsible, but also for what we do not do.*

MOLIÈRE
seventeenth-century French actor and dramatist

★ *If you aren't fired with enthusiasm, you will be fired with enthusiasm.*

VINCE LOMBARDI
one of the most successful coaches in National Football League history

★ *There is no excellence without difficulty.*

OVID
ancient Roman poet

★ *Make sure the thing you're living for is worth dying for.*

CHARLES MAYES

Work is man's great function. He is nothing, he can do nothing, he can achieve nothing, fulfill nothing, without working. If you are poor—work. If you are rich—continue working. If you are burdened with seemingly unfair responsibilities—work. If you are happy, keep right on working. Idleness gives room for doubt and fears. If disappointments come—work. When faith falters—work. When dreams are shattered and hope seems dead—work. Work as if your life were in peril. It really is. No matter what ails you—work. Work faithfully—work with faith. Work is the greatest remedy available for mental and physical afflictions.

AUTHOR UNKNOWN

The best thing to give an enemy is forgiveness;
To an opponent, tolerance,
To a friend, your ear;
To your child, a good example;
To a father, reverence;
To your mother, conduct that will make her proud of you;
To yourself, respect;
And to all, charity.

BENJAMIN FRANKLIN
eighteenth-century American statesman and philosopher

C O N S I D E R

What am I really aiming at?

How good am I really in comparison to my contemporaries in regard to:

★ Scholarship

★ Do I really understand about people, and am I able to get along with them?

★ Am I trying to make my body a useful instrument or am I neglecting it?

F. SCOTT FITZGERALD
From a letter to his daughter, Frances, 1933

Young people say, "What is the sense of our small effort?" They cannot see that they must lay one brick at a time; we can be responsible only for the one action at the present moment. But we can beg for an increase of love in our hearts that will vitalize and transform all our individual actions, and know that God will take them and multiply them, as Jesus multiplied the loaves and fishes.
DOROTHY DAY
twentieth-century American journalist

MONEY MATTERS

Balancing the Budget

There can be no freedom or beauty about a home life that depends on borrowing and debt.

HENRIK IBSEN
nineteenth-century Norwegian playwright

To secure a contented spirit, measure your desires by your fortunes, and not your fortunes by your desires.

JEREMY TAYLOR
seventeenth-century English prelate and author

Beware of little expenses; a small leak will sink a great ship.

BENJAMIN FRANKLIN
eighteenth-century American statesman and philosopher

Prosperity is only an instrument to be used; not a deity to be worshipped.

CALVIN COOLIDGE
thirtieth U.S. president

He who loves money shall never have enough. The foolishness of thinking that wealth brings happiness! The more you have, the more you spend, right up to the limits of your income, so what is the advantage of wealth—except perhaps to watch it as it runs through your fingers!

ECCLESIASTES 5:10–11 TLB

EVERY DOLLAR COUNTS

Tips for Managing Your Money

Create a budget and stick to it. Make sure your budget is a realistic reflection of your income and expenses. You can fudge on paper, but reality can't be fooled.

Record all transactions—checks *and* ATM withdrawals. It's a hassle to stop and write something down in your check register, but it's the only way to keep from nickel-and-diming yourself right into overdraft fees.

Balance your checkbook every month. There is no other way to accurately determine how much money you have in your account—the bank isn't always up to date with your spending. Ignore this wise word, and you will be watching as the bank gobbles up lots and lots of your hard-earned dollars.

Using cash is much simpler. You always know how much you have to spend, but don't forget that cash withdrawals must be recorded in the checkbook as well.

Avoid credit cards. It's good to have one card for building credit and emergency situations, but beware, lots of things look like emergencies but aren't.

Save, save, save. There is no better financial advice than to save as much as you can without becoming a stay-at-home, do-nothing miser. Start early and keep it up. You'll thank yourself when you're old and gray and traveling the world.

Give God His due. This is an acknowledgment that all you have belongs to God. Don't just give because someone says you have to. Give thought to when, where, and to whom you give.

The Few

Edgar Guest

twentieth-century American journalist and poet

The easy roads are crowded
And the level roads are jammed.
The pleasant little rivers
With the drifting folks are crammed.
But off yonder where it's rocky,
Where you get a better view,
You will find the ranks are thinning,
And the travelers are few.

Where the going's smooth and pleasant
You will always find the throng,
For the many, more's the pity,
Seem to like to drift along.
But the steeps that call for courage,
And the task that's hard to do
In the end result in glory
For the never wavering few.

P R A Y E R

We have to pray with our eyes on God, not on the difficulties.

OSWALD CHAMBERS
twentieth-century Scottish evangelist and devotional writer

When you pray, rather let your heart be without words than your words without heart.

JOHN BUNYAN
seventeenth-century English author

God speaks in the silence of the heart. Listening is the beginning of prayer.

MOTHER TERESA
twentieth-century Catholic nun and beloved humanitarian

Prayer draws us near to our own souls.

HERMAN MELVILLE
nineteenth-century American novelist

Prayer and doubt, do without. Pray and believe, humbly receive.

AUTHOR UNKNOWN

No race can prosper till it learns that there is as much dignity in tilling a field as in writing a poem.

BOOKER T. WASHINGTON
nineteenth-century American educator

He sticks through thick and thin— I admire such a man.

ABRAHAM LINCOLN
sixteenth U.S. president

Be prepared. You're up against far more than you can handle on your own. Take all the help you can get, every weapon God has issued, so that when it's all over but the shouting you'll still be on your feet. Truth, righteousness, peace, faith, and salvation are more than words. Learn how to apply them. You'll need them throughout your life. God's Word is an indispensable weapon. In the same way, prayer is essential in this ongoing warfare. Pray hard and long. Pray for your brothers and sisters. Keep your eyes open. Keep each other's spirits up so that no one falls behind or drops out.

EPHESIANS 6:13–19 MSG

A Practical Remedy for Fear

Linda Myers-Sowell

Do you have fears—those monstrous obstacles that hem you in and keep you from becoming all you can be? Victory may be more accessible than you think. Try doing what you're afraid to do! It's simple; it's practical; it works. I know because I tried it.

Up through high school I was a very timid person. I would rather have taken an F than stand up in front of the class and give an oral report. My mother would have me practice my reports out loud in front of a mirror. There in my room, I could give the report without looking at my notes. But when I went back into the classroom, I would clam up in fear, and the room would get blurry. Pronouncing the simplest words was a struggle. I would say the report so fast that sometimes teachers would stop me and ask me to slow down or, even worse, ask me to start over.

One year I was required to give an oral report or I would receive an F not just on the report but also on my report card for that quarter. I always enjoyed writing the reports and usually received a very good grade on the written portion. We were assigned to write a fictional story taken from historical fact. I wrote about Christopher Columbus and received an A. But when the day came to read my report to the class, I choked.

The teacher called my name, "Linda, it is your turn to give your oral report." He went on to tell the class, "Linda has written an excellent example of a fictional story based on history. Please listen carefully, and you will understand the assignment better."

I should have been filled with confidence after that introduction. Instead, I felt like I was frozen in my seat. When the teacher asked me again to come up in front of the class, I just shook my head no. After school I told the teacher about my fear and accepted an F on my report card. The teacher suggested I take a public-speaking class, but I couldn't imagine being forced week after week to stand up in front of other students to give a speech.

Through my teenage years, I did my best to avoid uncomfortable situations. I longed for the chance to be in a school play, but my fears kept me from the auditions. Instead, I volunteered for the makeup crew. When my friends talked about running for a school office, I volunteered to write their campaign speeches or make their posters. But my fears kept me from considering myself a candidate.

A year after high school, I ran into one of my former teachers. He asked me what I had been doing since graduation. I explained that I was attending college and majoring in English. Then he asked if I had overcome my fear of speaking in public.

"I haven't been required to do that yet this year," I told him.

"Everyone needs to learn to be in front of people, even for just a short period of time," he told me. "It comes with practice, Linda. Have you thought about taking a public-speaking class?"

As I continued going to college at night, one of my classes was assertiveness training. The instructor helped us to examine ourselves to find what kept us from overcoming our fears. We watched a biographical movie about a woman who had overcome many things in her past to become successful. She had a great fear of heights. Gradually the woman in the film worked at getting to the top of tall buildings to look down and flew in airplanes until she began to conquer her fears. The final goal she set for herself was to parachute out of an airplane. She screamed for several seconds as she fell toward the earth. She had managed to do the thing she feared most—but she wasn't finished tackling her fears. Her parachute drifted downward until she landed on a lake. It was a planned landing, and a boat quickly came to pick her up. But just before it arrived, she turned toward the camera and told the audience that she was also afraid of water and could not swim.

I found myself strangely inspired by the woman's actions. *If she could overcome her fears by challenging herself in this way, why can't I?*

I began to think of how I could push myself to go beyond what I had perceived were my limits. Meeting people and carrying on conversations were difficult for me. I read books about successful people and found that most people have to learn this art in order to initiate conversations. Studying topics of conversation became fun. Rehearsing in my mind what I would say seemed silly at first, but it also became a habit. Over time, my fear of new people and new surroundings began to diminish.

Finally, the day came when I enrolled in a public-speaking class. Each week we were assigned a different topic to talk about for five minutes. I saw what I should have known all along: everyone in the class had knees that were shaking and voices quivering. The first few speeches I gave, I thought I might pass out. My whole body and voice were shaking. After a few weeks, I began to volunteer to give my speech first. That way I could relax the rest of the class time and pay more attention to everyone else's speech. At the end of the semester, I received an A. But in order to be sure I was free—I registered for another semester of public speaking.

Now I'm able to stand up and give a talk anytime I am asked. My only regret is that I waited so long to confront my fear and conquer it—simply by doing what I feared most![20]

A N G E R

Get it under control

Anger is like the waves of a troubled sea; when it is corrected with a soft reply, as with a little strand, it retires, and leaves nothing behind but froth and shells—no permanent mischief.

JEREMY TAYLOR
seventeenth-century English prelate and author

Anyone can become angry. That is easy. But to be angry with the right person, to the right degree, at the right time, for the right purpose and in the right way—that is not easy.

ARISTOTLE
fourth-century B.C. Greek philosopher

A quick-tempered man starts fights; a cool-tempered man tries to stop them.

PROVERBS 15:18 TLB

The two best times to keep your mouth shut are when you're swimming and when you're angry.

AUTHOR UNKNOWN

BALANCE IN YOUR LIFE

No doubt about it, life comes at us like a freight train. It's hard to avoid being spun around and losing your bearings. But it can be done. Consider these tips:

☐ **Look deep inside and decide what matters most**. What is it you most want to accomplish—career, family, changing the world, etc.

☐ **Get rid of useless distractions.** This doesn't mean giving up TV or hanging out with your friends. It means identifying those things that pull you in a direction you don't want to go—unproductive obligations, rituals you don't care about.

☐ **Make time for yourself.** Too many people feel guilty for enjoying life. Don't let that happen to you. Those personal time-outs foster inner well-being and harmony as well as creativity.

☐ **Don't bite off more than you can chew.** Throwing yourself into things usually results in failure. Remember this ancient wisdom: the journey of a thousand miles begins with one step. You don't have to get it all done today. You have plenty of time to reach your goals.

☐ **Take care of your body.** Young people often have a false sense of immortality. Ask yourself: what good are my achievements if I don't live to enjoy them?

☐ **Invite God to take an active role in your life**. Remember that He knows the future and you don't.

THE CANONS OF PRACTICAL LIFE

Thomas Jefferson
third U.S. president

1. Never put off till tomorrow what you can do today.

2. Never trouble another for what you can do yourself.

3. Never spend your money before you have it.

4. Never buy what you do not want, because it is cheap; it will not be dear to you.

5. Pride costs us more than hunger, thirst, and cold.

6. We never repent of having eaten too little.

7. Nothing is troublesome what we do willingly.

8. How much pain they have cost us—the evils that have never happened.

9. Take things always by their smooth handle.

10. When angry, count to ten before you speak; if very angry, count to one hundred.

TEN POINTS TO REMEMBER

Abraham Lincoln
sixteenth U.S. president

1. You cannot bring about prosperity by discouraging thrift.

2. You cannot strengthen the weak by weakening the strong.

3. You cannot help small men up by tearing big men down.

4. You cannot help the poor by destroying the rich.

5 You cannot lift the wage earner up by pulling the wage payer down.

6. You cannot keep out of trouble by spending more than your income.

7. You cannot further the brotherhood of man by inciting class hatred.

8. You cannot establish sound social security on borrowed money.

9. You cannot build character and courage by taking away a man's initiative and independence.

10. You cannot help men permanently by doing for them what they could and should do for themselves.

GREAT BOOKS TO HELP YOU FIND YOUR WAY

As soon as you get out into the world, the first thing you're going to notice is that things aren't what you thought they were. You must educate your education. These seven books should help you do that.

☐ *What Color Is Your Parachute?* by Richard Nelson Bolles
How to apply your major to the real world

☐ *Do What You Are* by Paul D. Tieger and Barbara Barron-Tieger
Choosing a career based on personality type

☐ *Oh, the Places You'll Go* by Dr. Seuss
Preparing for a new phase of life

☐ *Saucepans & the Single Girl* by Jinx Morgan and Judy Perry
Practical advice with humorous commentary for young women starting out on their own

☐ *A Short Guide to a Happy Life* by Anna Quindlen
How to keep life, love, and work in balance

☐ *9 Things Graduates Must Do* by Henry Cloud
Learning what successful people have in common

☐ *The Holy Bible* by God
An essential read for anyone determined to succeed in life

One verse from Life's Lessons

Author Unknown

I learn, as the years fall onward,
And leave the past behind,
That much I have counted sorrow
But proves that my Lord was kind;
That many a flower I had longed for,
Had hidden a thorn of pain;
And many a rocky bypath
Led to fields of golden grain.

Praise the LORD, O my soul; all my inmost being, praise His holy name. Praise the LORD, O my soul, and forget not all His benefits—Who forgives all your sins and heals all your diseases, Who redeems your life from the pit and crowns you with love and compassion, Who satisfies your desires with good things so that your youth is renewed like the eagle's.

PSALM 103:1–5

I believe in God and in His wisdom and benevolence.
JOHN ADAMS
second U.S. president
from an 1818 letter to Thomas Jefferson

I compare the troubles which we have to undergo in the course of a year to a great bundle of sticks, far too large for us to lift. But God does not require us to carry the whole at once. He mercifully unties the bundle, and gives us first one stick, which we are to carry today, and then another, which we are to carry tomorrow, and so on. This we might easily manage, if we would only take the burden appointed for us each day; but we choose to increase our troubles by carrying yesterday's stick over again today, and adding tomorrow's burden to our load, before we are required to bear it.
JOHN NEWTON
eighteenth-century clergyman who wrote the hymn "Amazing Grace"

The best things in life are nearest: breath in your nostrils, light in your eyes, flowers at your feet, duties at your hand, the path of right just before you. Then do not grasp at the stars, but do life's plain, common work as it comes, certain that daily duties and daily bread are the sweetest things in life.
ROBERT LOUIS STEVENSON
nineteenth-century Scottish novelist

Ask me and I will tell you remarkable secrets you do not know about things to come.
JEREMIAH 33:3 NLT

Meet the Dream Weavers

*Am I unable to do certain
things, or am I simply
unwilling to invest the time
and effort necessary to succeed?*

Brett Harris

Rebelution? Yes, that is spelled correctly. The Harris twins, Alex and Brett, are leaders of a rebelution in America. They are rebelling, not against their parents or against the law, but against the low expectations today's culture holds for young men and women. No one seems to expect much of the teens in modern American culture, they say. Teenagers don't even expect much of themselves. Society not only expects little from young people but often expects only trouble from them. The Harris boys want to change that—to lead a revolt.

Alex and Brett coined the word *rebelution* from the words *rebellion* and *revolution*. Through their blogging, they preach a message to their generation. The message is clear: *You can do hard things! You should do more than is expected of you by our culture!* The two young men want to encourage young people to answer the call to be faithful to Christ and live a life that honors God. This has become the theme of their work. It is the title of their first book, *Do Hard Things: A Teenage Rebellion Against Low Expectations.*

These courageous brothers have led the rebelution through the development of their website, *TheRebelution.com,* founded in August 2005. The site has grown at an awesome rate to become one of the top Christian sites. The twins are probably among the most widely read writers on the web.

When the boys are not busy working on a political campaign, they are organizing and holding one-day conferences across the country for teens and parents. They also write for Focus on the Family's *Boundless* magazine. They have been featured on CNN, MSNBC, NPR, *World*, *Breakaway*, and *Ignite Your Faith* magazines, and even the *New York Times*.

Alex and Greg are the sons of one of the great homeschool pioneer couples, Gregg and Sono Harris. Their older brother, Joshua, is the bestselling author of *I Kissed Dating Goodbye*.

They love soccer, basketball, music, filmmaking, and politics. They plan to keep on with their blogging—leaders of a great Rebelution!

THE POWER OF POTENTIAL

Are you willing to do what it takes to achieve your dream? That's what God expects of you. He won't hand it to you with no effort, no struggle, no investment on your part. But He will walk with you every step of the way, helping you remove obstacles, overcome circumstances, and capture your dream.

Those who are wise shall shine like the brightness of the sky and those who lead many to righteousness, like the stars forever and ever.

DANIEL 12:3 NRSV

TIPS FOR GOOD HEALTH

For true success, you need a healthy body!

1. Wear your seat belt.
2. Get a checkup once a year.
3. Go to the dentist every six months.
4. Get an eye exam once a year.
5. Don't smoke.
6. Eat healthy and not to excess.
7. Take time to relax and go on vacation.
8. Find stress releasers in your day-to-day life.
9. Exercise three times a week.
10. Forgive those who offend you.
11. Accept who you are and what you can and cannot do.
12. Smile more than you frown.

To lengthen thy life, lessen thy meal.
BENJAMIN FRANKLIN
eighteenth-century American statesman and philosopher

Never lose an opportunity to see anything beautiful.
Beauty is God's handwriting.
CHARLES KINGSLEY
nineteenth-century English clergyman and novelist

A man will be what his most cherished feelings are. If he encourage a noble generosity, every feeling will be enriched by it; if he nurse bitter and envenomed thoughts, his own spirit will absorb the poison, and he will crawl among men as a burnished adder, whose life is mischief, and whose errand is death. He who hunts for flowers will find flowers; and he who loves weeds may find weeds.

HENRY WARD BEECHER
nineteenth-century American clergyman

A man should never be ashamed to own he has been in the wrong, which is but saying in other words, that he is wiser today than he was yesterday.

ALEXANDER POPE
eighteenth-century English poet

As long as you live, keep learning how to live.

SENECA
first-century Roman statesman, dramatist, and philosopher

Be Kind

Margaret Courtney
American poet

Be kind to thy father—for when thou wert young
Who loved thee so deeply as he?
He caught the first accents that fell from thy tongue,
And joined in thine innocent glee . . .

Be kind to thy mother—for lo! on her brow
May traces of sorrow be seen;
Oh, well mayst thou cherish and comfort her now
For loving and kind hath she been! . . .

Be kind to thy brother—wherever you are
The love of a brother shall be
An ornament purer and richer by far
Than pearls from the depths of the sea.

Be kind to thy sister—not many may know
The depth of true sisterly love,
The wealth of the ocean lies fathoms below
The surface that sparkles above.
Thy kindness shall bring to thee many sweet hours
And blessings thy pathway to crown,
Affection shall weave thee a garland of flowers
More precious than wealth or renown.

Four Things

Henry van Dyke
twentieth-century American pastor and educator

Four things a person must learn to do
If he would make his record true:
To think without confusion clearly;
To love his fellowmen sincerely;
To act from honest motives purely;
To trust in God and Heaven securely.

Take time to think: it is the source of power.
Take time to play: it is the secret of perpetual youth.
Take time to read: it is the fountain of wisdom.
Take time to laugh: it is the music of the soul.
Take time to give: it is too short a day to be selfish.
AUTHOR UNKNOWN

ATTITUDE

It's a matter of choice.

☐ Today I can complain because the weather is rainy, or I can be thankful that the grass is getting watered for free.

☐ Today I can feel sad that I don't have more money, or I can be glad that my finances encourage me to plan my purchases wisely and guide me away from waste.

☐ Today I can grumble about my health, or I can rejoice that I am alive.

☐ Today I can lament over all that my parents didn't give me when I was growing up, or I can feel grateful that they allowed me to be born.

☐ Today I can cry because roses have thorns, or I can celebrate that thorns have roses.

☐ Today I can mourn my lack of friends, or I can excitedly embark upon a quest to discover new relationships.

☐ Today I can whine because I have to go to work, or I can shout for joy because I have a job to do.

☐ Today I can complain because I have to go to school, or I can eagerly open my mind and fill it with rich new bits of knowledge.

☐ Today I can murmur dejectedly because I have to do chores around the house, or I can feel honored because the Lord has provided shelter for my mind, body, and soul.

Today stretches ahead of me, waiting to be shaped. And here I am, the sculptor who gets to do the shaping. What today will be like is up to me. I get to choose what kind of day I will have!

From Self-Reliance

Ralph Waldo Emerson
nineteenth-century American essayist and poet

There is a time in every man's education when he arrives at the conviction that envy is ignorance; that imitation is suicide; that he must take himself for better for worse as his portion; . . . It is the harder because you will always find those who think they know what is your duty better than you know it. It is easy in the world to live after the world's opinion; it is easy in solitude to live after our own; but the great man is he who in the midst of the crowd keeps with perfect sweetness the independence of solitude.

THE POWER OF POTENTIAL

Today stretches ahead of you, waiting to be shaped. And you are the sculptor who gets to do the shaping. What today will be like is up to you. What will you choose for today?

Anyone who stops learning is old, whether at twenty or eighty.

HENRY FORD
twentieth-century innovator and manufacturer of American cars

_____

_____

_____

_____

_____

_____

Wise Words

Sir Winston Churchill
twentieth-century British statesman

I have no secret. You haven't learned life's lesson very well if you haven't noticed that you can give the tone or color, or decide the reaction you want of people in advance. It's unbelievably simple. If you want them to smile, smile first. If you want them to take an interest in you, take an interest in them. If you want to make them nervous, become nervous yourself. If you want them to shout and raise their voices, raise yours and shout. If you want them to strike you, strike first. It's as simple as that. People will treat you like you treat them. It's no secret. Look about you. You can prove it with the next person you meet.

Dear Graduate,

The truth is, as you shall soon learn, that taking one more step from childhood into adulthood requires the acceptance of responsibility but not the change of your personality. You will be the same person on the inside that you always were. If you like a certain kind of candy, you will not stop liking that candy. What you treasure will still be treasured, and what you like to do, you will still like doing. You will still have "toys" and want to play with them, but they will grow and change with you and your bank account.

Love,

A Graduate Who Has Gone before You

Recognize Opportunities

Mary Elizabeth Bain
American author

Despite the fact that the age in which we live is the freest, and our civilization is the richest in the world's history, there are everywhere those who magnify the past, who proclaim that the golden age has passed, and that today there are no battles to be fought, no triumphs to be gained. Blind to the new possibilities of life, their ears closed to the voice of action, they fold their hands and journey down to their graves with nothing attempted and nothing achieved. "Impossible" is their cry, and yet all the luminous deeds of this world have been done in spite of their cries.

It is true that science has revealed many wonderful secrets. She has read the stories upon the rocks, laid hold upon the stars, and penetrated nature's mysteries. But even now, for the aspiring person, she has still greater mysteries to divulge.

True, the fundamental principles of law have been expounded, but with our complex civilization, new questions clamor forth for answers, more wrongs cry to be righted, and more crimes need to be prosecuted.

True, another Caesar may not win his fame or with iron hand rule the world, yet, whether living in a palace or a hovel where the poor congregate, opportunity is everywhere for the person of will, nerve, and soul to write his name among the stars.

There may never be another Washington, but there are opportunities for the truehearted to catch inspiration from his noble life and drive tyrants from our shores, in order to place God's banner triumphant over the walls of sin.

In this age, when every man may become a king, every woman a queen and yet none wear a crown! To those who are really seeking an opportunity to develop the best there is in them.

To those who seek possibilities, opportunities rise in every wind, sing in every breeze, smile in every atom, and are locked in every cell. For them, every dewdrop is a force to turn their spindle, every breath of air an energy to drive their ship, every sunbeam a power to energize their machine. To hopeful, ambitious people, every day is a chance to demonstrate their worth, every hour an opportunity to show their power, every second a time in which rise to them ultimate possibilities.

It is true that some doors have been closed. There are yet others unlocked, behind which are hidden treasures. Diamonds have been found in mother earth, but there are still brighter gems. Waterloos have been won on fields of blood, but greater battles are yet to be won on fields of peace. The earth has been girdled with electric wires, but it is yet unrimmed by Christian civilization.

There are latent, in every heart, songs as yet unsung, anthems as yet unheard, chords which, if but struck, would fill this old world of ours with music, thrill the soul of man with joy, string his heart and nerves with strength, exalt his life with hope, sweeten it with gladness, and set his whole being tingling with nobleness and love.

There are fruits as yet unplucked, sweeter than honey and more beautiful than the sight of sun-kissed grapes. There are books yet unread, and leaves yet uncut in the life of every person. There are rewards waiting for those who conquer difficulties, utilize their talents, and invest their untold worth.

For all who strive, who are willing to use untried forces, unknown energies, there are ungathered riches, unheard harmonies, unwon crowns, and yes, unrevealed heaven.

Things Worth Remembering

Author Unknown

The value of time
The success of perseverance
The pleasure of working
The dignity of simplicity
The worth of character
The improvement of talent
The influence of example
The obligation of duty
The wisdom of economy
The virtue of patience
The joy of originating

To look up and not down;
To look forward and not back;
To look out and not in;
And to lend a hand.

EDWARD EVERETT HALE
twentieth-century clergyman, editor, and humanitarian

AUTHENTIC MAKEOVER

True Beauty

☐ For attractive lips, speak words of kindness.

☐ For beautiful eyes, seek out the good in other people.

☐ For better hearing, listen to the Word of God.

☐ For poise, walk with knowledge and self-esteem.

☐ For strong arms, hug at least three people a day.

☐ For a strong heart, forgive yourself and others.

☐ For a good life, walk this earth lightly and yet leave your mark.

AUTHOR UNKNOWN

Most people forget God all day and ask Him to remember them at night.

AUTHOR UNKNOWN

It's easier to fight for one's principles than to live up to them.

ALFRED ADLER

twentieth-century psychologist who studied human behavior

Rules for Human Relationships

E u s e b i u s
fourth-century theologian and church historian

May I be no man's enemy.

May I be a friend of that which is eternal and abides.

May I never quarrel with those nearest to me.

If I do, may I be reconciled quickly.

May I love, seek, and attain only what is good.

May I wish for all men's happiness and envy no one.

May I never rejoice in the ill fortune of someone who has wronged me.

May I win no victory that harms either me or my opponent.

How far you go in life depends on your ability to be:
Tender with the young,
Compassionate with the aged,
Sympathetic with the striving,
Tolerant of the weak and strong.
Someday in your life you will have been all of these.
GEORGE WASHINGTON CARVER
American botanist

THE POWER OF POTENTIAL

Never let your ambition cause you to step on others. What can you do today to help someone else be successful?

Live among men as if the eye of God was upon you;
Pray to God as if men were listening to you.

SENECA
first-century Roman statesman, dramatist, and philosopher

Human beings, should esteem Love, embrace Humility, and grasp Peace.

HILDEGARD OF BINGEN
twelfth-century German abbess, monastic leader, author, and composer

The art of living is more like wrestling than dancing.

MARCUS AURELIUS
second-century Roman emperor

The Little Clock

Author Unknown

There's a neat little clock,
On its high shelf it stands,
And it points to the time
With its two little hands.

May we, like the clock,
Keep a face ever bright,
With hands ever ready
To do what is right.

A new life begins for us with every second. Let us go forward joyously to meet it. We must press on, whether we will or not, and we shall walk better with our eyes before us than with them ever cast behind.

JEROME K. JEROME

nineteenth-century English humorist, novelist, and playwright

One of the hardest lessons we have to learn in this life, and one that many persons never learn, is to see the divine, the celestial, the pure, in the common, the near at hand—to see that heaven lies about us here in this world.

JOHN BURROUGHS

nineteenth-century American naturalist

Meet the Dream Weavers

I touch the future. I teach.

Christa McAuliffe

Teachers influence our future. During children's school-age years, they arguably spend more time with their teachers than their parents. Christa McAuliffe, the tragic, accidental astronaut, was keenly aware of her responsibility to her students and considered teaching her God-given gift.

Born in Boston, Massachusetts, in 1948, Christa grew up in nearby Framingham. After graduating from high school, she earned a degree in history from Framingham State College and then a master's degree in education from Bowie State College in Maryland.

A dedicated junior-high teacher, Christa taught history, social studies, and civics. She also volunteered at her church, led a Girl Scout troop, and raised funds for a hospital and the YMCA.

In 1984, Vice President George H.W. Bush announced the newly inaugurated "Teacher in Space Project." Two months later, McAuliffe filed her application. She explained her reason for applying:

I remember the excitement in my home when the first satellites were launched. I was caught up with their wonder. I cannot join the space program and restart my life as an astronaut, but I watched the Space Age being born, and I would like to participate.

The initial process narrowed the applicants to 114 and then 10. Finally, by a unanimous decision, McAuliffe was chosen out of 11,500 applicants to be the first private citizen included in a space mission.

In her classes at school, Christa taught that history is a result of "ordinary people living their lives in their own times." Her desire, as the first civilian in space, was to "humanize the space age by giving the perspective of a non-astronaut." As part of the deal, she agreed to keep an extensive journal of an "everyday teacher" in space. Her mission caught the fancy of students around the country, who enthusiastically followed her progress.

On January 28, 1986, the seven-member crew of the *Challenger* space shuttle lifted off. On the aircraft, McAuliffe carried a T-shirt that read, "I touch the future. I teach." Though tragically the shuttle exploded seventy-three seconds later, killing all on board, Christa McAuliffe proved that day that in life and death she could touch the future.

In everything set them an example by doing what is good. In your teaching show integrity, seriousness and soundness of speech.

TITUS 2:7–8

THE POWER OF POTENTIAL

Try to imagine two ways that you can touch the future with your life and gifts.

For all sad words of tongue and pen, the saddest are those "It might have been."

JOHN GREENLEAF WHITTIER
nineteenth-century American poet

BE HAPPY

Tips for Living a Happy Life

1. Count your blessings, not your troubles.

2. Learn to live one day at a time.

3. Learn to say, "I love you," "Thank you," and "I appreciate you."

4. Learn to be a giver and not a taker.

5. Seek the good in everyone and everything.

6. Pray every day.

7. Do at least one good deed every day.

8. Put God first.

9. Don't let yourself get hot and bothered.

10. Practice the "Do it now" habit.

11. Fill your life with goodness.

12. Learn to laugh, and learn to cry.

13. Don't worry; be happy.

14. Learn to fear nothing and no one.

15. Learn to let go and let God.

For the joy of the LORD is your strength.
NEHEMIAH 8:10

To love what you do and feel that it matters—how could anything be more fun?
KATHARINE GRAHAM
twentieth-century publisher

AUTHENTIC RELATIONSHIP WITH GOD

Tips for Keeping Your Relationship with God Fresh and Alive

At some point each person has to decide what his or her relationship with God will look like—faith has to become personal. It cannot be your parents' faith or your pastor's faith. It has to be your faith. These tips will help you discover God in a personal way and maintain a strong, vital relationship with Him:

- ☐ **Acknowledge who He is.** God is more than a higher being responsible for creating the earth. He is your Creator and wants to be your heavenly Father, your Helper, your Savior.

- ☐ **Acknowledge who you are.** You are a sinner, in need of saving. And you are loved by God, always have been and always will be.

- ☐ **Reach out to Him.** The first time is to ask for forgiveness and to be washed clean from your sins. After that, reach out countless times each day to access His love, His wisdom, and His strength.

- ☐ **Read His Word.** The Bible is much more than a book. It is a letter to you from God. Read it daily to keep your relationship growing and flourishing.

- ☐ **Pray, pray, pray.** When you pray, you are talking to God, interacting with Him. Communication is the most important factor in any relationship.

- ☐ **Spend time with people who love God.** Never underestimate your need for fellowship, fresh perspective, and insight.

Life's Tug of War

Author Unknown

Life can seem ungrateful and not always kind.
Life can pull at your heartstrings and play with your mind.
Life can be blissful and happy and free.
Life can put beauty in the things that you see.
Life can place challenges right at your feet.
Life can make good of the hardships we meet.
Life can overwhelm you and make your head spin.
Life can reward those determined to win.
Life can be hurtful and not always fair.
Life can surround you with people who care.
Life clearly does have some ups and some downs.
Life's days can bring you both smiles and frowns.
Life teaches us to take the good with the bad.
Life is a mixture of happy and sad.

Take the life that you have and give it your best.
Think positive, be happy, let God do the rest.
Take the challenges that life has laid at your feet.
Take pride and be thankful for each one you meet.
To yourself give forgiveness if you stumble and fall.
Take each day that is dealt you and give it your all.

Take the love that you're given and return it with care.
Have faith that when needed it will always be there.
Take time to find beauty in the things that you see.
Take life's simple pleasures; let them set your heart free.
The idea here is simply to even the score.
As you are met and faced with life's Tug of War.

Life is a journey, not a destination.
AUTHOR UNKNOWN

*In three words I can sum up everything
I've learned about life: It goes on.*
ROBERT FROST
beloved twentieth-century American poet

*Life is a daring adventure,
or it is nothing.*
HELEN KELLER
twentieth-century American deafblind lecturer and author

The Great Danger

Phillips Brooks

nineteenth-century American bishop who wrote "O Little Town of Bethlehem"

The great danger facing all of us is not that we shall make an absolute failure of life, not that we shall fall into outright viciousness, nor that we shall be terribly unhappy, nor that we shall feel that life has no meaning at all—not these things. The danger is that we may fail to perceive life's greatest meaning, fall short of its highest good, miss its deepest and most abiding happiness, be unable to tender the most needed service, be unconscious of life ablaze with the light of the Presence of God—and be content to have it so—that is the danger: that some day we may wake up and find that always we have been busy with husks and trappings of life and have really missed life itself.

For life without God, to one who has known the richness and joy of life with Him, is unthinkable, impossible. That is what one prays one's friends may be spared—satisfaction with a life that falls short of the best, that has in it no tingle or thrill that comes from a friendship with the Father.

The value of life lies not in the length of days, but in the use we make of them.
MICHEL DE MONTAIGNE
sixteenth-century French essayist

Today!

Author Unknown

With every rising of the sun
Think of your life as just begun.
The Past has cancelled and buried deep
All yesterdays. There let them sleep.

Concern yourself with but Today.
Grasp it, and teach it to obey
Your will and plan. Since time began
Today has been the friend of man.

You and Today! A soul sublime
And the great heritage of time.
With God himself to bind the twain.
Go forth, brave heart! Attain ! Attain!

W I S D O M   S P E A K S

I feel overwhelmed. Sometimes I want to turn back time. Would it be so wrong to just continue doing what I'm doing and hope everything turns out for the best?

Action springs not from thought, but from a readiness for responsibility.

DIETRICH BONHOEFFER
twentieth-century German religious leader and fighter against Nazism

To live means to have a mission to fulfill—and in the measure in which we avoid setting our life to something, we make it empty.

JOSÉ ORTEGA Y GASSET
twentieth-century Spanish philosopher, writer, and statesman

The soul that has no established aim loses itself.

MICHEL DE MONTAIGNE
sixteenth-century French essayist

The tragedy of life doesn't lie in not reaching your goal. The tragedy lies in having no goal to reach. It isn't a calamity to die with dreams unfulfilled, but it is a calamity not to dream. It is no disgrace to not reach the stars, but it is a disgrace to have no stars to reach for. Not failure, but low aim, is a sin.

BENJAMIN MAYS
twentieth-century minister, scholar, social activist, and college president

Sometimes I get so upset at my family, teachers, and others. I feel like they did not prepare me for this next step. Am I right to feel this way?

Being unready and ill-equipped is what you have to expect in life. It is the universal predicament. It is your lot as a human being to lack what it takes. Circumstances are seldom right. You never have the capacities you ought to have. You must always do with less than you need in a situation vastly different from what you would have chosen as appropriate for your special endowments.

CHARLTON OGBURN JR.
twentieth-century American author

A secure individual knows that the responsibility for anything concerning his life remains with himself—and he accepts that responsibility.

HARRY BROWNE
American libertarian writer

How am I supposed to follow God in everything when I have no idea what I'm doing now?

God does not ask the impossible, but instructs you to do what you are able, and to pray for aid in doing what you are not able to do yourself, that He may help you.

DECREES OF THE COUNCIL OF TRENT

The Lord still waits for you to come to Him, so He can show you His love; . . . For the Lord is faithful to His promises. Blessed are all those who wait for Him to help them.

Isaiah 30:18 TLB

The Art of Happiness

Author Unknown

There was never a time when so much official effort was being expended to produce happiness, and probably never a time when so little attention was paid by the individual to creating the personal qualities that make for it. What one misses most today is the evidence of widespread personal determination to develop a character that will in itself, given any reasonable odds, make for happiness. Our whole emphasis is on the reform of living conditions, of increased wages, of controls on the economic structure—the government approach—and so little on man improving himself.

The ingredients of happiness are so simple that they can be counted on one hand. Happiness comes from within and rests most securely on simple goodness and clear conscience. No one is known to have gained it without a philosophy resting on ethical principles. Selfishness is its enemy; to make another happy is to be happy oneself. It is quiet, seldom found for long in crowds, most easily won in moments of solitude and reflection. It cannot be bought; indeed money has very little to do with it.

No one is happy unless he is reasonably well satisfied with himself, so that the quest for tranquility must of necessity begin with self-examination. We shall not often be content with what we discover in this scrutiny. There is so much to do, and so little done. Upon this searching self-analysis, however, depends the discovery of those qualities that make each man unique and whose development alone can bring satisfaction.

Of all those who have tried, down through the ages, to outline a program for happiness, few have succeeded so well as William Henry Channing:

"To live content with small means; to seek elegance rather than luxury, and refinement rather than fashion; to be worthy, not respectable, and wealthy, not rich; to study hard, think quietly, talk gently, act frankly; to listen to the stars and birds, to babes and sages, with open heart; to bear all cheerfully, do all bravely, await occasions, hurry never; in a word, to let the spiritual, unbidden, and unconscious grow up through the common."

It will be noted that no government can do this for you; you must do it for yourself.

THE POWER OF POTENTIAL

Do you desire happiness? What are you going to do to attain it?

I'm just as happy with little as with much, with much as with little. I've found the recipe for being happy whether full or hungry, hands full or hands empty. Whatever I have, wherever I am, I can make it through anything in the One who makes me who I am.

PHILIPPIANS 4:12-13 MSG

THE TEN COMMANDMENTS

FOR GRADUATES

1. **Thou shalt not forget that graduation is the *beginning* of your education.**
   Education begins the gentleman; but reading, good company, and reflection, must finish him.
   JOHN LOCKE
   seventeenth-century English philosopher

2. **Thou shalt decide your path by learning from the mistakes of others.**
   Employ your time in improving yourselves by other men's documents; so shall you come easily by what others have labored hard for. Prefer knowledge to wealth; for the one is transitory, the other perpetual.
   SOCRATES
   ancient Greek philosopher

3. **Thou shalt not let fear or doubt keep you from pursuing your dreams.**
   It is idleness that creates impossibilities; and where men care not to do a thing, they shelter themselves under a persuasion that it cannot be done. The shortest and the surest way to prove a work possible, is strenuously to set about it, and no wonder if that proves it possible that, for the most part, makes it so.
   ROBERT SOUTH
   seventeenth-century English clergyman

4. **Thou shalt focus on where you are going, rather than complaining about your life.**
   Murmur at nothing. If your ills are reparable, it is ungrateful; if remediless, it is vain.
   CHARLES CALEB COLTON
   nineteenth-century English cleric, writer, and collector

5. **Thou shalt not neglect others as you pursue your dreams.**
He that does good to another man does also good to himself; not only in the consequence, but in the very act of doing it; for the consciousness of well doing is an ample reward.
SENECA
first-century Roman statesman, dramatist, and philosopher

6. **Thou shalt remember that your work is important because it affects the lives of others.**
If we work upon marble, it will perish; if we work upon brass, time will efface it; if we rear temples, they will crumble into dust; but if we work upon immortal minds, if we imbue them with principles, with the just fear of God and love of our fellowmen, we engrave on those tablets something which will brighten to all eternity.
DANIEL WEBSTER
nineteenth-century American statesman and orator

7. **Thou shalt not live for yourself but for God.**
The Lord your God told me to give you all these commandments which you are to obey in the land you will soon be entering, where you will live. The purpose of these laws is to cause you, your sons, and your grandsons to reverence the Lord your God by obeying all of His instructions as long as you live; if you do, you will have long, prosperous years ahead of you.
MOSES IN DEUTERONOMY 6:1–2 TLB

8. **Thou shalt keep your eyes on God, and He will keep His eyes on your path.**
He that provides for this life, but takes no care for eternity, is wise for a moment, but a fool forever; and acts as untowardly and crossly to the reason of things as can be imagined.
JOHN TILLOTSON
seventeenth-century English prelate and archbishop of Canterbury

9. **Thou shalt not try for even one moment to be what you are *not*!**

The man who will live above his present circumstances is in great danger of living, in a little time, much beneath them.

JOSEPH ADDISON
seventeenth-century English essayist, dramatist, and poet

10. **Thou shalt follow advice, learn from your mistakes, and enjoy your life.**

Experience keeps a dear school, but fools will learn in no other and scarcely in that; for it is true we may give advice but we cannot give conduct. Remember this; they that will not be counseled cannot be helped. If you do not hear reason, she will rap your knuckles.

BENJAMIN FRANKLIN
eighteenth-century American statesman and philosopher

There is no more blessed way of living,
than the life of faith upon a covenant-keeping God.
To know that we have no care, for he cares for us;
That we need have no fear, except to hear him;
That we need have no troubles, because we have
cast our burdens upon the Lord,
and are conscious that he will sustain us.

C. H. SPURGEON
England's best-known preacher of the nineteenth century

BE ALERT

Tips for Staying Safe

After graduation, you may be living on your own for the first time. That can be exciting, offering a new level of independence. But it can also be a bit frightening at times, especially if you were used to having a lot of people around at home or in a dorm. Consider these tips for playing it safe when you're on your own:

☐ **Do your homework.** I know what you're thinking, but homework will always be part of life! Choose where you live carefully. Look for lighted parking areas, well-lit corridors, and safety locks on doors and windows. And pay attention to where your new digs are located.

☐ **Meet your neighbors.** You'll want to know who you can call on if you need help and be able to identify strangers.

☐ **Take responsibility for your own safety.** Locks don't do any good unless you use them. Don't hang around outside after dark. Lock your car. Be aware of your surroundings. Don't open the door to strangers. Don't give your personal information to people you don't know well.

☐ **Organize a neighborhood watch.** This is a good idea even for apartment dwellers. Watching out for each other just makes sense.

☐ **Check in every day with someone**, anyone who will be concerned if she doesn't hear from you.

Great Truths from Unknown Thinkers

Confidence is the companion of success.

To know how to laugh is to know how to reign.

The secret of success in conversation is to be able to disagree without being disagreeable.

The three primary principles of wisdom: obedience to the laws of God, concern for the welfare of mankind, and suffering with fortitude all the accidents of life.

If there is righteousness in the heart, there is beauty in the character. If there is beauty in the character, there will be harmony in the home. If there is harmony in the home, there will be order in the nation. When there is order in the nation, there will be peace in the world.

With most people, lovability is not absent—it is merely undiscovered.

The heritage of the past is the seed that brings forth the harvest of the future.

An ounce of loyalty is worth a pound of cleverness.

Nothing is impossible for the valiant heart.

Clear water flows from a pure spring.

The greatest men are the simplest.

The good you do is not lost though you forget it.

He who has a thousand friends has not one to spare.

Where God gives, envy cannot harm, and where He gives not, all labor is in vain.

To know where you can find a thing is in reality the best part of learning.

Patience and perseverance surmount every difficulty.

Consideration is the parent of wisdom.

The giver makes the gift precious.

Do what thou lovest; paint or sing or carve.
Do what thou lovest, though your body starve!
Who works for glory oft may miss the goal.
Who works for money merely starves the soul;
Work for the work's sake, then, and it may be,
these other things will be added unto thee.

References

Notes

1. Edith Painton, *The Commencement Manual* (Chicago: Beckley-Cardy Company, 1943, 57–61.

2. "Fork in the Road" by Sue Rhodes Dodd. Used by permission of the author.

3. "Long Division" by Alison Simpson. Used by permission of the author.

4. "YOU Write the Songs" by Bonnie Compton Hanson. Used by permission of the author.

5. "Fired by Design" by Rebekah Montgomery. Used by permission of the author.

6. "Say Cheese" by Kinberly J. Fish. Used by permission of the author.

7. "You Mud, You Tape, and You Keep Going" by Nancy Hoag. Used by permission of the author.

8. "A Change of Plans" by Coleen P. Kenny. Used by permission of the author.

9. "Ballerina Dreams and Beautiful Realities" by Alison Simpson. Used by permission of the author.

10. "Love Settles the Question" by Sharon Gibson. Used by permission of the author.

11. "Just Listen" by Sue Rhodes Dodd. Used by permission of the author.

12. "The Right Job for Me!" by Jean Wensink. Used by permission of the author.

13. Jeanne Gowen Dennis, *Running Barefoot on Holy Ground: Childlike Intimacy with God* (Grand Rapids: Kregel Publications, 2006). Used by permission of the author.

14. "My Dream Job It Wasn't!" by LeAnn Campbell. Used by permission of the author.

15. "Lord, What Is Your Plan for Me?" by Linda Myers-Sowell. Used by permission of the author.

16. "Bloom" by Taprina Milburn. Used by permission of the author.

17. Jeanne Gowen Dennis, *Running Barefoot on Holy Ground: Childlike Intimacy with God* (Grand Rapids: Kregel Publications, 2006). Used by permission of the author.

18. "Stronger Than You Think" by Brenna Fay Rhodes. Used by permission of the author.

19. "Unidirectional Showers" by Matthew Kinne. Used by permission of the author.

20. "A Practical Remedy for Fear" by Linda Myers-Sowell. Used by permission of the author.